101 ADORABLE BREEDS

dogs

RACHAEL HALE

Andrews McMeel
Publishing, LLC
Kansas City

Introduction

I feel hugely privileged that in my career as an animal photographer I've had the opportunity to meet all sorts of dogs: big and small; shy and gregarious; elegant and scruffy. Although already a dog lover, I have developed an even greater love and respect for these gorgeous creatures. Each dog I have photographed—no matter what the breed and despite any so-called "imperfections"—has been an utter character in its own right. Just as dogs don't care what their owners look like, what really matters about a dog is what's on the inside; which in my experience is affection and personality by the bucketful.

While not intended as a complete reference, this compendium of lovable canines includes a great range of popular breeds. You may find it useful if you're planning to buy a dog; or perhaps it will prove the perfect present for a dog-loving friend. Whatever your intention, I hope that each portrait provides as much joy in the viewing as I experienced in the creating.

Contents

Hound

1. Afghan Hound

The Afghan Hound is an aristocratic, dignified, and somewhat aloof breed with a very loyal and affectionate nature. It is a breed of significant antiquity, believed to have existed in ancient Egypt, and depicted in cave drawings in northern Afghanistan that date from over 4,000 years ago. The elegant sight-hound was used in Afghanistan as both shepherd and hunter, due to its versatility, speed, agility, and stamina. It was adept at hunting wolves, jackals, marmots, and snow leopards. Afghan Hounds were first introduced to the Western world in the nineteenth century, and today the breed has become a luxurious pet known for its noble and majestic beauty. It is often referred to as "a king of dogs."

Appearance: The Afghan Hound is tall and slender, with a long, narrow, refined head. Its long silky topknot, distinctive coat pattern, and very prominent hip-bones, large feet, and dark almond-shaped eyes give the Afghan Hound its exotic appearance.

Color: A large range of colors is seen, although Afghan Hounds are predominantly sand colored, with a darker face and ear fringes.

2. Basenji

Elegant, agile, and intelligent, the graceful Basenji is widely known as the "barkless dog." Prized for their speed, hunting power, and silence, they are known to have existed in ancient Egypt but were only discovered by Western civilization in Africa during the late nineteenth century. Their balanced and refined muscle structure enabled them to achieve fast and agile movement, and this combined with an independent and brave nature to produce a fine hunting dog. Although valued for their silence during a hunt, the dogs actually have an amazing vocabulary of sounds—the most common being a happy yodel. Although sometimes aloof with strangers, the Basenji is friendly and calm among friends and lovingly protective with children. They are fastidious in their habits, and are known to clean themselves in a similar fashion to cats.

Appearance: The Basenji is a small, short-haired dog with a distinctive wrinkled head. An arched neck and curled tail set high add to its elegant and alert appearance. The Basenji is short backed and lightly built, so that it appears tall for its length. The breed is known for its swift, effortless gait, similar to a racehorse in full trot.

Color: A variety of colors including chestnut red, pure black, tricolor (black and red), and brindle (black stripes against chestnut red). All have white feet, chest, and tail tip, with possible white on the legs, blaze, and collar.

3. Basset Hound

A good-natured though slightly stubborn dog, the Basset Hound originated in France—the name derives from the French adjective "bas," meaning "low." Long a popular dog throughout Europe, the Basset Hound was used primarily as a hunting dog. Unlike other hunters, the Basset is small of stature, a characteristic developed by the friars of the French abbey of St. Hubert, making the dogs easily followed on foot. A great scent hunter, second only to the Bloodhound, the Basset Hound has a low-slung body and long nose that trails the ground closely. Its size and build allow for easy movement through dense bush, and the breed's stamina and determination enable the dogs to travel long distances in search of quarry, typically hare and rabbit. Graceful and obedient, with a loving and cheerful nature, Basset Hounds enjoy the company of children and make fine family companions.

Appearance: The Basset Hound is short legged and heavy boned, with a large chest and lungs, as befits a hunting dog. It has a short, smooth but loose coat, with exaggeratedly long ears and drooping eyelids that give it a slightly forlorn appearance.

Color: The Basset typically appears black, white, and tan, or lemon and white.

4. Beagle

Active, cheerful, and intelligent, the Beagle is known for its friendly temperament and great hunting ability. Although there are no reliable records of the Beagle's early history, it is accepted that pack hounds were introduced to England before Roman times and form the basis of both sight and scent hounds. The increased popularity of foxhunting and subsequent breeding of foxhounds during the eighteenth century led to the development of the Beagle. The Foxhound, a cross of Buck Hound and Beagle, produced two distinct types of dog: the Southern Hound and the North Country Beagle. This Beagle strain was successfully introduced into America in the 1860s, and it is still used today to hunt in packs. Beagles also make excellent companions and great family dogs. They enjoy the company of children, and have an endearingly playful and upbeat, sometimes boisterous nature. They also have the advantage of an easily cared-for coat, compact size, and remarkable lack of doggy odor.

Appearance: The Beagle is a solid and compact dog that resembles the Foxhound, although it is smaller in size. It has tough forelegs and tight feet, and on average ranges in height from 1 to 1¼ feet.

Color: Beagles present in a range of colors, the most common being black, tan, white, and a combination of the tricolor. They can also be tan and white or lemon and white.

5. Bloodhound

The Bloodhound is an extremely affectionate, responsive, and sensitive dog. Developed carefully to keep the breed's strain pure, the Bloodhound is so named to reflect the aristocracy of the breed, not the object they hunt. Theirs is an ancient lineage, believed to date back to the Roman Empire, when their ancestors were renowned for their unrivalled power of scent and great stamina. The Bloodhound was first brought into Europe from Constantinople (now Istanbul) as two strains, and the modern Bloodhound is a cross of the two. The hound's tracking ability was first trialled by the British police in 1805, and today the breed holds a highly respected place in law enforcement, with the accuracy of its tracking accepted in most courts. A tireless worker, the Bloodhound is also extremely affectionate and gentle. Although somewhat shy, these dogs enjoy the company of children and other pets. They are also very protective, and make good watchdogs.

Appearance: Larger than most hounds, the powerful Bloodhound is well designed for scent hunting. The hound's deep chest gives it a good lung capacity and the large ears are believed to sweep the scent up into its large nostrils. The skin is thin to the touch and loose, hanging in deep folds around the head and neck.

Color: The Bloodhound is typically two-toned, appearing as either black and tan or liver and tan. White can be present on the chest, feet, and tip of the stern, or tail.

6. Borzoi

Of Russian descent, Borzoi were bred for many centuries as aristocratic hunting dogs. Although long-hunting hounds are mentioned during the reign of Genghis Khan in the thirteenth century, it was not until 1650 that the first Borzoi standard was written. Originally known as Russian Wolfhounds, they are a mix of Arabian Greyhounds and an ancient thick-coated Russian breed. Since they were designed to hunt wolves, special emphasis was placed on a strong neck and powerful jaw capable of snatching and holding their catch. Relying on sight rather than scent, the Borzoi is capable of running at tremendous speed and shows great courage and agility when working. During the 1860s, when hunting was the favored sport of the nobility, it was common to see hunting packs of over a hundred Borzoi. Although still used to control wild game, they are more prized today for their aristocratic beauty and keen intelligence than for their innate hunting ability. Borzoi have a gentle nature, enjoy the company of people, and are especially playful with children.

Appearance: Refined and elegant, Borzoi are tall hounds with a highly developed muscular build. A lean and long head supported by a slightly arched but powerful neck runs into sloping shoulders and a strong body.

Color: Any color or combination of colors.

7. Dachshund

The Dachshund, an energetic, intelligent, and brave dog, was developed in Germany from the fifth century, primarily to hunt badgers. Illustrations dating from three hundred years ago show badgers being pursued by dogs with elongated bodies, low to the ground, with hound-like ears. Eventually named the Dachshund in reference to their hunting role ("Dachs" meaning badger; "Hund" meaning dog), they were known to have the tracking ability of hounds and the stature and nature of terriers. The Dachshund breed comes in three coat varieties: smooth-, long-, and wire-haired. Early in the development of the Dachshund group, German breeders realized that crossing between the different varieties was detrimental, and it was subsequently banned. However, the dogs were eventually bred in both standard and miniature sizes. Dachshunds are smart, active, and courageous, and they make friendly and devoted family companions.

Appearance: The Dachshund is well balanced and low to the ground. It has short legs, with strong forequarters and forelegs, and a long body. All versions should have a bold head shape, with a confident and intelligent expression.

Color: The Dachshund presents in all colors.

8. Greyhound

The handsome Greyhound is considered to be the oldest pure breed known, and there is little doubt that the dogs depicted in ancient carvings and literature are the same as the Greyhounds of today. Their history can be traced back to Egypt around 2900 BC, when Greyhound types attacking deer and mountain goats were carved on the Tomb of Amten. Between 43 BC and AD 17, the Roman writer Ovid wrote the first comprehensive description of the breed. These pieces of historical evidence present Greyhounds across numerous continents, and show them to be acclaimed hunters of practically all types of game from deer to foxes and hares. Lithe, muscular, and light footed, with far-reaching sight, Greyhounds are well-designed hunters that are able to cover ground at great speed. During the nineteenth century, when coursing clubs and sport racing became increasingly popular, Greyhounds became the sport's preferred racer, stamping the image of the Greyhound and mechanical hare on history. With their instinctive sense of the chase, Greyhounds make wonderful active family pets. Even tempered and sweet natured, they are extremely loyal and very affectionate.

Appearance: The Greyhound is strongly built, with a muscular body and powerful legs, and a symmetrical appearance. The long head and neck emphasize the breed's long-reaching movement, great speed, and immense stamina.

Color: Greyhounds can be any color, with black, white, red, and blue being most favored.

9. Harrier Hound

Cheerful, sweet tempered, and outgoing, the Harrier Hound enjoys company and has a love of exploring. The Harrier originated in Britain in the thirteenth century to serve hunters of hare. Tireless workers with a well-developed sense of smell, they hunted in packs and were favored because they were able to be followed on foot. Eventually the Harrier became known as a poorer man's dog, due to its prevalence in the "scratch pack," where a hunting pack was made up of hounds owned by numerous individuals. Although there is a suggestion that the Harrier developed from the old Southern Hound, with the addition of a little Greyhound blood, it is widely believed that the Harrier is simply a smaller version of the Foxhound, bred down in size by selective breeding. What is agreed upon is the Harrier's playful nature and friendly temperament. They work well with other dogs and enjoy a life full of people, dogs, or both, and their tolerant nature makes them a great companion for children.

Appearance: The Harrier has all the qualities of a scenting packhound. Well balanced, with a muscular build, it exudes great stamina and strength. Essentially it is a smaller version of the English Foxhound.

Color: A variety of hound colors.

10. Irish Wolfhound

An ancient breed of the Greyhound variety, the Irish Wolfhound is the tallest of all dogs. Referred to in early Irish literature as Wolfdogs or Great Hounds of Ireland, these gentle giants were once celebrated hunters of the local wolf, wild boar, and the large Irish elk. They were exclusively owned by the nobility, as their huge size made it virtually impossible for peasants to be able to feed them. With dwindling numbers of adequate game for the large dogs, Captain George A. Graham is credited with saving the breed from demise. In 1862 he began a breeding program that twenty-three years later resulted in the first breed standard for the Irish Wolfhound. Although formidable in size, they have an extremely friendly nature and are without suspicion, making the breed completely unsuited to any role as a guard- or watchdog. They are, however, extremely loyal and love constant companionship.

Appearance: The Irish Wolfhound, the largest and tallest of the galloping hounds, is an imposing sight. Muscular but gracefully built, these dogs combine power and agility. A proudly carried head and rather long neck is balanced by an upward-sweeping, slightly curved tail.

Color: Gray, brindle, red, black, pure white, fawn, or any deerhound color.

11. Rhodesian Ridgeback

The Rhodesian Ridgeback is the only known breed to come from South Africa. Early South African literature tells us of a native hunting dog that was half wild, with a ridge down its back. During the sixteenth and seventeenth centuries, immigrants brought a new mixture of breeds to South Africa, mainly Danes, Mastiffs, Greyhounds, Terriers, and Bloodhounds. These breeds naturally mixed with the indigenous hunting dogs and produced the foundation stock of the Rhodesian Ridgeback we know today. In 1877 two Ridgebacks were introduced into Rhodesia, where they became famous for their exceptional ability in the sport of lion hunting. In 1922 Rhodesian fanciers established the breed standard, giving the dogs their name. Also referred to as the African Lion Hound, Ridgebacks are more than just exceptional hunting dogs. Intelligent, courageous, and cunning, they are extremely devoted to their owners and show great loyalty, kindness, and affection.

Appearance: Handsome and dignified, Rhodesian Ridgebacks are strong, muscular, and well balanced dogs that are capable of good speed and great endurance. The signature ridge on the back is formed from the hair growing in the opposite direction to the rest of the short, dense coat.

Color: Light wheaten to red wheaten, with white markings on the chest and toes.

12. Saluki

The elegant Saluki is considered the oldest known domesticated breed of dog. The earliest known carvings depicting Saluki-like dogs come from excavated sites of the Sumerian Empire, and date from around 7000–6000 BC. From there they travelled to Egypt, Persia, India, and Afghanistan, where they were considered the "royal dog of Egypt." The dogs were so exalted that their bodies were often mummified. Admired for their tremendous speed, they were talented sight hunters of the gazelle. Being highly valued, they were often presented as gifts to important Europeans and eventually found their way to Europe around the twelfth century. However, it was not until 1840 that they appeared in England, where they became known as Persian Greyhounds and were used to hunt foxes and hares. Their aristocratic appearance is coupled with a far-reaching expression, as if they are looking into the distance, which certainly reflects their exceptional sight. Although lightly built, they are admired for their tough and hardy character, and they are known to be extremely loyal to those they trust.

Appearance: Symmetrically built and slender, carrying little fat, Salukis have powerful thigh muscles and long feet. They exude an appearance of elegance, grace, and great speed.

Color: White, cream, fawn, golden, red, grizzle and tan, tricolor (white, black, and tan), and black and tan.

13. Whippet

A beautiful and graceful breed, Whippets are the fastest domesticated dogs of their weight, with speeds of up to 34 mph recorded. Whippets were developed as racing dogs when the barbaric sports of bullbaiting and dogfighting lost their popularity and a new form of entertainment was sought. Originally named "snap-dogs" after the action of snapping up the prized rabbit that drove them to race, they were also nicknamed "the poor man's racehorse," a direct reference to the purely gaming nature of their role. For animals with such an ignoble history, Whippets are a refined and elegant-looking dog. In contrast to their energetic and racy nature outside, they are quiet and very charming at home. Dignified and gentle, their amicable personality disguises their superb hunting ability.

Appearance: Conveying an image of speed and power combined with grace and elegance, Whippets are a true sporting hound. Symmetry of outline and a muscular physique are accentuated by a short, smooth, and close coat. The head is long and lean, with bright eyes and an intelligent expression.

Color: Any color or mixture of colors.

Herding

14. Australian Cattle Dog

The Australian Cattle Dog is a loyal, hard-working dog with a strong protective instinct. It was developed by crossing the native dingo and a mix of working dogs brought to Australia from England. Breeders were finally successful with the Scottish blue merle/Highland Collie mix in 1840. These dogs proved excellent workers, and inspired further breeding with the imported Dalmatian, producing a dog that was fearless around horses and loyal to its master, with the speckle blue or red coat for which the Australian Cattle Dog is famous. In the search for a breed with still greater working ability, the dogs were further crossed with the Black and Tan Kelpie, a sheepdog. The high-quality pups that emerged are recognized as the bloodline of the present breed. The result was an ideal farming dog—compact and active like the dingo, loyal and friendly like the Dalmatian, and hard working like the Kelpie. Now indispensable to the farming community, the Australian Cattle Dog is highly valued for its courage, intelligence, dedication, and devotion.

Appearance: Developed specifically to work in both expansive and confined farmland, these dogs are strong and compact looking. They are symmetrically built, with strong muscular character, and are surprisingly agile.

Color: Well known for their unusual markings, which are found on no other dog in the world. Their coat is either speckled blue or red.

15. Australian Shepherd

The Australian Shepherd is a medium-sized dog known for its loyalty, intelligence, and stamina. Despite its name, the Australian Shepherd is an exclusively American-bred dog. Its ancestors are believed to have originated in the Basque region, between Spain and France, and to have been brought by Basque shepherds to the United States via Australia during the 1800s. Affectionately referred to as the "Aussie," the Australian Shepherd was a favored dog of the ranchers of the American West. The breed's adaptable, easily pleased nature, and their receptiveness to training, has led to their wide use, and they are still employed today as ranch working dogs. They are acclaimed blind dogs, pet-therapy dogs, drug detectors, and search and rescue dogs.

Appearance: An athletic-looking dog, well balanced and agile. Its body is slightly longer than it is tall, and covered by a medium-length coat.

Color: The Australian Shepherd comes in a variety of colors including black, blue merle, red, and red merle. White or tan markings may be present on the face, chest, front, and rear legs.

16. Bearded Collie

One of Britain's oldest breeds, the exuberant, happy-go-lucky Bearded Collie was bred for both companionship and work. Affectionately called the "Beardie," the breed is also known as the Highland Collie, the Mountain Collie, or the Hairy Mou'ed Collie. Like most shaggy-haired herding dogs, the breed is believed to descend from the Magyar Komondor of Central Europe, from which it was developed into a hardy, active, and agile herder. Following a time of great popularity during the Victorian era, the breed nearly disappeared, but was kept alive by the Peebleshire shepherds of Scotland, who valued its qualities as a great working sheepdog. Over time the self-confident and intelligent Beardie has steadily regained popularity, and today these dogs are highly regarded as loving family members.

Appearance: The Beardie is a strong, muscular dog of medium size, long and lean, with a bright, inquisitive expression. The Beardie has a medium-length shaggy coat and comes complete with a beard, from which it takes its name.

Color: Born either black, blue, brown, or fawn, with or without white markings. As the dogs age, their coat changes from dark to light. White markings can appear as a blaze on the foreface, on the skull, tip of the tail, chest, legs and feet, and around the neck.

17. Border Collie

Independent and intelligent, with immense stamina and endurance, the Border Collie is recognized as the world's premier sheep herding dog. Affectionate toward friends, its protective instincts serve it well in caring for its master's herds. Although it is known to have originated in the border country of England and Scotland, the exact history of the breed is unclear. However, the Scottish dialect word "collie" confirms its direct link to the rugged Scottish landscape, which helped develop the breed's unique working style of wide sweeping outruns. The Border Collie was admired by Queen Victoria and became an increasingly popular companion dog, until eventually reinstated as a leading sheep herder when sheep dog trials began in London in 1876, where spectators were amazed at the breed's obedience, intelligence, and athleticism.

Appearance: The Border Collie is a medium-sized dog with an athletic body typically covered by a moderately long coat. It has a fairly broad head, and an alert and intelligent expression.

Color: Black and white is by far the most common color combination, with black tricolor (black, tan, and white) and red and white blends also seen regularly. Blue and white, red merle, blue merle, "Australian red," and sable are less common.

18. Briard

Often described as "a heart wrapped in fur," the Briard is an ancient French working dog that can be seen in tapestries dating from the eighth century. Originally used as herding dogs, they would also loyally defend their charges against predators and poachers. Their intelligence and willingness to learn make them extremely versatile dogs, and throughout history Briards have been used in a variety of roles. In addition to tracking and hunting, their acute hearing, excellent memory, and determined courage meant they were valuable war sentries and search and rescuers as well as loyal companions for patrolling soldiers. When love and affection are freely given in large doses, Briards respond reciprocally with immense devotion and loyalty. They are very popular companion dogs, gentle and obedient, with a love of play that can become rough. Wary of strangers, they can be very effective guard dogs.

Appearance: Distinctive hairy eyebrows that arch up and down lightly covering the eyes, a full beard, and a coarsely textured coat give the Briard its characteristic rugged appearance. Strong and muscular of body, they are sound athletically and powerful herding specimens. A key characteristic of the Briard is the two dewclaws on each rear leg.

Color: Black, various shades of gray, and tawny, with a combination of these colors possible.

19. German Shepherd Dog

Loyal, courageous, and intelligent, the German Shepherd Dog (often called the Alsatian) is renowned for its great endurance, strength, and willingness to be trained and worked. Initially developed as a German herding and farm dog, today the breed is one of the most popular and recognizable of dogs. The German Shepherd excels in many roles, and they are prized as blind dogs, drug dogs, search and rescue, police, and service dogs. An immensely loyal breed, they are known to be "one-man" dogs—they do not give their love away easily, but once given, it is given for life. They will defend fearlessly and display high levels of intelligence, patience, and, to a certain degree, the exercise of judgment.

Appearance: The German Shepherd Dog has a powerful and well-muscled build that is well suited to endurance and speed, and quick and sudden movements. It is a well-proportioned dog, appearing slightly longer than tall, strongly boned, with an outline of smooth curves rather then angles. It has a double coat of medium length.

Color: The German Shepherd Dog appears in a variety of colors, the most common being black, black and tan, and sable.

20. Old English Sheepdog

The Old English Sheepdog is intelligent and affectionate, with a great love of children. Indeed, they are known to use their innate herding skill to gently nudge together those under their care. Although not of great antiquity, as suggested by its name, the breed can be found around 150 to 200 years ago. It was developed in the west of England around the beginning of the nineteenth century, with most experts believing that either the Scotch Bearded Collie or the Russian Owtchar had an important place in its lineage. Although originally used to herd sheep and cattle, the Old English Sheepdog makes an ideal house dog. Its calm, friendly, and adaptable nature, combined with the ability to be easily trained, makes it well suited to families.

Appearance: Old English Sheepdogs are easily recognized by their characteristic profuse and shaggy coats. Surprisingly, they are no harder to care for than any other long-haired breed. Beneath the coat the dog is strong, compact, and squarely built. It has a distinctive shuffling gait, rather like a bear, and an impressively loud bark.

Color: Any shade of gray, grizzle, blue, or blue merle, with or without white markings, or the reverse.

21. Pembroke Welsh Corgi

The Pembroke Welsh Corgi is a separate breed to the original Cardigan Corgi, and today is the more popular of the two. Believed to be the younger of the Corgi types, the Pembroke Welsh Corgi is still no young puppy. Early in the twelfth century, Flemish weavers, who were also efficient farmers, settled in Wales with the ancestors of the breed. They also used the bold and agile Pembrokes as herding dogs, and the breed's droving abilities are still admired and used today. Intelligent and alert, affectionate yet never demanding of attention, the Pembroke was at home inside the Flemish farmhouse and typically found guarding the prized spot in front of the fire. Their popularity increased in Britain after the Duke of York gave his daughter Princess Elizabeth (later Queen Elizabeth II) a Pembroke puppy in 1933. Today they are much-loved family pets and can still be found guarding the fireside.

Appearance: The Pembroke Welsh Corgi is a sturdy and strongly built dog, appearing longish in body, with a bright, keen expression. It has a short, thick, weather-resistant coat.

Color: Red, sable, fawn, or black and tan, with or without white markings on the legs, chest, neck, muzzle, underparts, and head.

22. Puli

A vital part of the Hungarian herding landscape for over a thousand years, the Puli were celebrated for their agility, vigor and, versatility. Descended from the sheepdogs of the Magyar, who settled in Hungary, and similar to the Tibetan Terrier, the original Puli was nearly lost when Hungary was invaded in the sixteenth century and numerous imported strains of sheepdog were introduced. It was not until 1912 that a pure Puli-breeding program was established, and two distinct coats appeared: shaggy and curly. Their innate droving ability means they are as at home on the hills as inside, where they make an affectionate and devoted companion. They are excellent watchdogs, while their bouncy and active nature makes them a lot of fun to have around and perfect family dogs.

Appearance: The Puli is easily recognized, with its unique shaggy, weather-resistant coat (there is nothing like it in dogdom). The coat appears dense and profuse, and if left to develop naturally forms cords. Underneath is a body of medium size that is square and compact.

Color: Solid colors of black, rusty black, all shades of gray, and white.

23. Rough Collie

Originating in Scotland and northern England, the forebears of the Rough Collie were hard-working farm dogs, used primarily for guiding cows and sheep to market. The breed's name probably derives from one of their known charges—the Scottish black-faced sheep called the Colley. Prior to the nineteenth century, Collies were strictly working dogs with no written pedigrees, but by 1886 a breed standard was well established and the Rough Collie split from other shepherding breeds such as the Border Collie. The breed has been popular since the time of Queen Victoria, much admired for its dignified and elegant appearance. Rough Collies are loyal and affectionate, and have a particular affinity with children. Highly intelligent and easily trained, they make perfect family companions.

Appearance: The Rough Collie is a handsome breed, strong and active, standing straight and firm with a distinctive lion-like, abundant coat. Well balanced, with a deep, moderately wide chest, the Rough Collie presents a picture of pride and grace.

Color: The Rough Collie can appear in a range of colors, the four most common being sable and white, tricolor, blue merle, and white.

24. Shetland Sheepdog

Loyal and extremely respectful, the Shetland Sheepdog is one of the most successful obedience dogs. Naturally willing to obey, an instinct developed over many generations of well-trained dogs, they are essentially a working Collie in miniature. Believed to be descended from the Scottish Rough Collie and the Icelandic Yakkin, the breed has changed little since the eighteenth century. Developed as a herder and protector of sheep in the rugged landscape of the Shetland Islands, their small size is reflected in many of the animals of the isolated islands. Shetland Sheepdogs have a natural desire to guard, and their size and agility allows them to chase swiftly and gracefully, making them efficient working farm dogs and hunters. At the same time, their intense loyalty and immense affection make them very much a family dog. They are cheerful by nature and enjoy the company of children, who they will protect faithfully.

Appearance: The Shetland Sheepdog is a miniature Rough Collie, with noted differences of size and coat. Its body is small and symmetrical, while the coat is long, rough, and abundant. These characteristics, combined with an expression of sweetness, make the Shetland Sheepdog a very attractive dog.

Color: Sable, blue merle, and black, all marked with varying amounts of white and/or tan.

Working

25. Alaskan Malamute

A powerful, dignified, and loyal dog, the Alaskan Malamute is one of the oldest of the Arctic sled breeds. Early references to the breed came from sailors returning from the upper western shores of Alaska, who spoke of dogs driving sledges for the native Inuit people of the area, the Mahlemuts, whose name was later given to the breed. The dogs were possibly bred with others brought over by the white settlers. Further mixing occurred when sled racing became popular, and faster, lighter dogs were sought. With the rise of sled racing in the United States, there was increased interest in retaining the pure breed, with emphasis on the Malamute's strength and stamina, rather than speed. A pure strain of Alaskan Malamute was acknowledged in 1926. The Malamute is a friendly, sociable dog that enjoys company. The dogs' high-energy, playful nature, and loyal devotion make them loving companions.

Appearance: The Malamute is handsome and dignified, standing well over the pads, with powerful shoulders, an erect head, alert eyes, and sharp pointed ears. Built to pull heavy loads, its muscular body is the heaviest of any of the sled dogs. The coat is short and dense.

Color: Malamutes can be any shade of gray through to black, sable, and shadings of sable to red. White markings cover the underbelly, mask, legs, and feet.

26. Bernese Mountain Dog

The handsome Bernese Mountain Dog is an affectionate and intelligent breed. Easily recognized, with their tricolored long, silky coat, they are one of four varieties of Swiss Mountain Dog known in their native land as Berner Sennenhund. Brought into Switzerland over 2,000 years ago by the invading Romans as watchdogs, the Bernese were bred by locals for farm work. Their strength and agility were perfect for navigating the treacherous mountain passes, and they became celebrated drovers and draft dogs. Although at one point almost lost, the breed was re-established by a single Swiss fancier, Franz Schertenleib, who in 1892 worked loyally to protect and revive it. Today they are recognized as loving and loyal companions, with a cheerful, intelligent, and willing nature.

Appearance: The Bernese Mountain Dog has an aristocratic appearance, with a distinctive tricolor coat that is long and silky. It is sturdy boned, and slightly longer in the body than tall. The eyes are almond-shaped, dark brown, and expressive, adding to their natural appearance of self-confidence.

Color: The tricolored mix is made up of black, rich rust, and white. The ground color is jet black, with rust highlights over each eye, wrapping the corners of the mouth and cheeks, framing the chest, on all four legs, and the underside of the tail. The white forms the blaze, muzzle band, and chest.

27. Boxer

Although bred for protection, the Boxer has an endearing playfulness and patience that makes it a treasured working dog and family member as well as a committed guard dog. A medium-sized dog developed in Germany, the Boxer was originally descended from the ancient fighting dog of Tibet, and contains strains of Bulldog and Terrier. It was favored by German breeders for its protective nature and courage, and was the first breed to be used in the German police force. However, in developing the Boxer, breeders managed to retain the dog's original qualities while establishing a more attractive specimen. Today's Boxers have an instinctively protective nature combined with great devotion and loyalty. They are intelligent and trainable, and show great courage and strength.

Appearance: The Boxer is a medium-sized, squarely built dog, short-haired, with strong limbs and a muscular body. The chiseled head, with its broad, blunt muzzle, is the most distinctive feature of the Boxer. In body it epitomizes strength, agility, and refinement, all qualities of a specifically developed top-quality guard and working dog.

Color: Boxers are typically either fawn or brindle. They often have a white underbelly, chest, and feet, with white occasionally showing on the face. Fawn shades range from light tan to mahogany. Brindle varies from thin and clear stripes on a fawn coat to heavy striping.

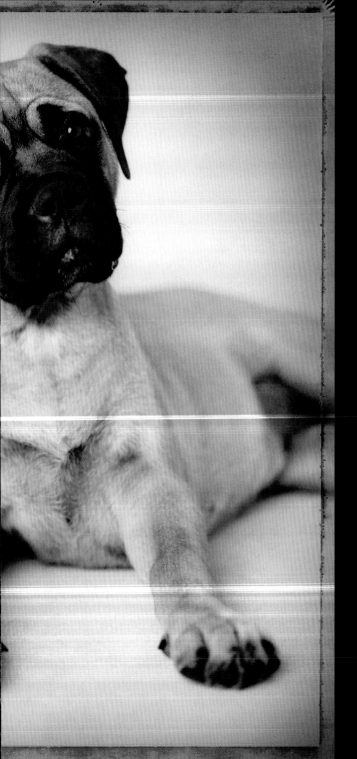

28. Bullmastiff

The Bullmastiff, an intelligent and loyal dog, was bred in the nineteenth century to protect English gameland from poachers. It was developed by crossing the Mastiff, which was considered too slow and lacking in aggression, with the Bulldog, itself small and too ferocious. The Bullmastiff was highly prized for its courage, speed, and agility, as well as its ability to attack on command and hold its prey without mauling. The dogs' intelligence and willingness to serve led to their use with the army and police forces. Today Bullmastiffs are valued family companions, known for their firm, dependable, and warm natures.

Appearance: The Bullmastiff is a powerfully built, muscular dog, with a short, dense coat. An adult male will average just over 2 feet in height and weigh 120 pounds. The head, with its longer nose and powerful jaw, is reminiscent of the ancient Bulldog.

Color: Red, fawn, or brindle.

29. Doberman Pinscher

The Doberman was developed in Germany in the late nineteenth century as a medium-sized dog that would be both protector and companion. It is believed to be a mix of old short-haired shepherd, Rottweiler, Black and Tan Terrier, and German Pinscher. The breed was further refined by American fanciers, and officially recognized in 1900. An intelligent, powerful dog with great speed and stamina, the Doberman excels when mentally and physically stimulated. Suspicious of strangers, watchful, and fearless, Dobermans are very effective watchdogs, while their loyalty and obedience make them loving and dedicated companions.

Appearance: The Doberman is a medium-sized, compact, and muscular dog with a dignified carriage. Clean, powerful lines, a soft expression, and a short, smooth, close-lying coat all combine to make an extremely elegant dog.

Color: Most commonly black, with rust coloring above the eye, on the muzzle, throat, and fore-chest, all legs and feet, and below the tail. Other colors are red, blue, and fawn.

30. Great Dane

The elegant and distinguished-looking Great Dane is a true giant among dogs. It is a very old breed—dogs resembling the Great Dane can be found in Chinese literature as far back as 1121 BC, and huge dogs are pictured in Egyptian tombs around 3000 BC. However, it was during the Middle Ages that the breed was refined and developed in Germany. Bred to hunt Europe's most savage and powerful boars, the original Great Dane was notably vicious, and it was not until the breed was introduced to the United States in 1887 that American fanciers transformed it into a charming and good-natured dog. The Great Dane's sharp intelligence and protective instinct make it a celebrated guard dog, while its friendly, loyal, and dependable nature means it enjoys constant companionship.

Appearance: The Great Dane is an elegant and regal dog, strongly built, well formed, and very muscular. It moves with a long reach and powerful drive, giving an impression of briskness that is never clumsy. The coat is short, dense, and sleek.

Color: Brindle, fawn, blue, black, mantle, and harlequin.

31. Neapolitan Mastiff

An ancient breed believed to be descended from the giant war dogs of antiquity, the Neapolitan Mastiff has been directly linked to the Molossus, developed by Alexander the Great (356–323 BC) and used as a fighting dog, pitted against tigers, lions, elephants, and even man. The modern Neapolitan is believed to have been developed in Italy, primarily as a protector of home and estate, and retaining the giant size, heavy loose skin, and dewlap of the early dogs. A courageous defender of land and property, the Neapolitan Mastiff is extremely loyal and attacks only on command. It is a calm, easygoing breed that thrives as part of a family.

Appearance: The Neapolitan is a massive, heavy-boned dog that can weigh over 150 pounds. It is characterized by loose skin over the entire body, with plenty of hanging wrinkles and folds on the head, and a large dewlap. The dog's movement is rolling and lumbering, rather than elegant.

Color: Solid colors in various shades of gray (blue), black, mahogany, and tawny, with some brindling possible.

32. Newfoundland

A huge cuddly bear of a dog, the Newfoundland's most important characteristic is its sweet temperament and gentle way with people. The original dogs are believed to have been brought to the coast of Newfoundland, Canada, by European fishermen, and possibly bred with a Husky forebear. Used to haul carts and carry loads on land, Newfoundlands are also superior water dogs, being used in rescue work and to drag in nets. Their webbed feet help them to swim at speed, and their great strength and stamina make them natural lifesavers in the water. This work demands a high level of intelligence and self-confidence, but they are also a dog with an immense capacity to love, and they show great loyalty and devotion to their adopted family.

Appearance: The Newfoundland is a large, well balanced dog, heavily boned and muscular. It has a heavy double coat that has an oily feel to it, well suited to the water.

Color: Black, brown, gray, and white with black markings.

33. Saint Bernard

The Saint Bernard was named after Archdeacon Bernard of Menthon, who founded the famous hospice in the Swiss Alps where travelers passing between Switzerland and Italy were offered refuge. Brought to the hospice in the mid-seventeenth century, the dogs were companions to the monks, watchdogs over the hospice, and invaluable search and rescue dogs in the isolated and treacherous landscape. Over the past three centuries, their powerful sense of smell has enabled them to rescue over 2,000 people, and by the mid to late nineteenth century they had become famous worldwide. These large, powerful dogs, which can adapt to both warm and cold climates, are also extremely gentle and loving animals. They are very good with children and are particularly trustworthy, making them all-around family and companion dogs.

Appearance: A powerful and muscular dog, with a massive head and large feet, the Saint Bernard appears tall, bulky, and imposing. It has an intelligent expression, with eyes that are small and quite deep-set. There are two varieties: the shorthair, which has a smooth coat, and the longhair, with a rough coat.

Color: Red, brindle, brown-yellow with white markings, or white with red markings.

34. Samoyed

Cheerful and affectionate, the Samoyed is sometimes referred to as the "Laughing Cavalier" or the "smiling dog." The Samoyed is one of the truest modern breeds, with no crossbreeding evident. They are descended from the companion dogs of the ancient Iranian tribe, the Samoyed, who settled in the icy terrain of northern Siberia. The dogs lived a nomadic life, shepherding, driving sleighs, and providing companionship. The Arctic conditions bleached their coats white, and their flat feet are perfectly adapted to the icy landscape. They are hard workers and have been used successfully in the great Arctic and Antarctic expeditions, including that of Roald Amundsen in 1911. Their long relationship with humans has seen the Samoyed develop an almost "human" understanding, and their happy-go-lucky, almost childlike attitude makes them most endearing. Playful and mischievous, they have great affinity with children.

Appearance: Although beautiful and graceful, the Samoyed is essentially a working dog. It has a strong, muscular body, deep chest, and strong loins. It is instantly recognizable, with its heavy white, weather-resistant coat and typically cheerful expression.

Color: Pure white, white biscuit, or cream.

35. Siberian Husky

Siberian Huskies are well known as endurance sled dogs. They are descended from the working dogs of the Chukchi people of northeastern Asia, which over 3,000 years ago were primarily used to pull sleds and herd reindeer. Extremely versatile and hardy, these dogs were able to travel vast distances at moderate speeds and carry light loads in cold conditions without great exertion. The breed remained pure through to the nineteenth century when they were taken to Alaska. As the sport of sled racing grew in Alaska, so did the dogs' popularity, and they were officially recognized and named the Siberian Husky in 1939. Their incredible stamina and well-mannered disposition saw them serve courageously in the American Army Arctic Search and Rescue Unit during World World II and the Byrd Antarctic expeditions. These handsome dogs are sociable and friendly even to strangers. Intelligent and hardworking, with a delightful personality, they love being exercised and enjoy family life.

Appearance: The Siberian Husky is the image of power, speed, and endurance. It is medium sized, with a compact, muscular body and a distinctly wolf-like head. The remarkable almond-shaped eyes can be any color, even one brown and the other blue.

Sporting

36. American Cocker Spaniel

The American Cocker Spaniel is the smallest in the Sporting Group of "Cockers." It was originally developed from careful breeding of the English Cocker Spaniel. References to the large spaniel family are found as early as the fourteenth century, when the breed came to be divided into water and land spaniels. The "Cockers" were the smaller of the two types, and today the breed is one of the most popular purebred dogs in America. These dogs have been bred for their hunting, tracking, and retrieving ability, as reflected in their name—the word "cocker" refers to the woodcock, a gamebird these spaniels flushed particularly well. Cocker Spaniels are capable of considerable speed, combined with great endurance. An ideal family companion, they love to please, and their temperament is typically described as "merry."

Appearance: American Cocker Spaniels have a compact and sturdy body with a refined head, expressive eyes, and pendulous ears. They are distinctly different in appearance from their English counterparts. The head is shorter in the muzzle, with fuller eyes, and the coat is exaggeratedly long. They weigh an average of 17 to 28 pounds.

Color: There are numerous color varieties within the Cocker breed: black, black with tan points, partial color, and any solid color other than black.

37. Brittany

The happy-go-lucky Brittany takes its name from the French province in which it originated. It is an ancient breed, believed to have existed as early as AD 150, and precise details of its development are undocumented. However, it is believed that the Brittany is likely to have been bred along similar paths to the Welsh Springer Spaniel, and that the two were quite possibly interbred, which would explain the similarities in their appearance. Actual evidence of the breed does not appear until the seventeenth century, when Brittany dogs began to be depicted in paintings and tapestries. Written record of hunting dogs believed to be the Brittany—dogs with small bobtails, which worked well pointing and retrieving—appeared in 1850. These energetic dogs were recognized as a breed in 1907 and their natural hunting ability, moderate size, and happy temperament has seen their popularity soar. Always alert and ready for action, they make cheerful and affectionate family members.

Appearance: Compactly built and rather long in the legs, the Brittany is designed for great agility and speed. They characteristically appear tailless or with a docked tail, and have dense wavy or flat coats.

Color: Can appear in all colors and mixes of colors, with the most popular being orange and white or liver and white, with either clear or roan patterns.

38. Chesapeake Bay Retriever

The tale of the Chesapeake Bay Retriever is linked to an English shipwreck off the coast of Maryland in 1807. Rescued from the sinking ship were two puppies, a female and a male Newfoundland.

It was from these two dogs, which were admired for their impressive retrieving skills on the water, that the Chesapeake Bay Retriever developed. The offspring of the dogs were crossed with local retrieving dogs, as well as other crosses such as the English Otterhound, the Flat-coated Retriever, and the Curly-coated Retriever. The result was a breed that was celebrated for its stamina and agility in the cold waters around Chesapeake Bay, where the dogs could retrieve anywhere from 100 to 200 ducks a day, sometimes having to break through ice to complete the retrieve. Not only are Chesapeake Bay Retrievers intelligent and strong-minded dogs, they are highly loyal and devoted companions. They have a quiet good sense and are admired for their bright and happy temperament, making them exceptional family dogs.

Appearance: These agile, vigorous, and powerfully built dogs have been well-designed for extreme icy conditions. Strong and well balanced in body, they are covered by a superbly effective coat: naturally oily, the short, harsh outer coat covers a dense, fine, wool undercoat.

Color: Any brown variant from dark brown to faded tan or a dull straw color.

39. Curly-coated Retriever

Although the exact origin of the Curly-coated Retriever is unclear, it is believed to be the oldest of the retriever breeds. It is thought to have descended from crosses of English Water Spaniel, Saint John's Newfoundland, and the Retrieving Setter in the sixteenth century, which were mixed with the Poodle around the end of the nineteenth century. It was a favorite retriever of English gamekeepers, unsurpassed in the water, and celebrated for its natural field ability, great agility and speed, bravery, and immense stamina. Friendly and affectionate, the Curly-coated Retriever loves being around people. An active, intelligent breed with a great love of swimming and a charming and gentle nature, it is easy to get along with, loyal, and eager to please.

Appearance: The Curly-coated Retriever is easily recognized by its characteristic waterproof coat, which is made up of tight, crisp curls. These cover the bulk of the body, extending to the tail, while a smooth, short, straight coat covers the face, front of forelegs, and feet. It is a confident and aristocratic-looking breed, with a powerful build, and appears taller then other retriever breeds.

Color: Black or liver.

40. English Cocker Spaniel

The English Cocker Spaniel, one of the oldest spaniel breeds, is well known for its happy-go-lucky, cheerful temperament. Until the seventeenth century all spaniels were grouped together, and it was not until 1892 that the English Kennel Club finally acknowledged individual breeds, based on hunting ability and size. Prior to this, Springer Spaniels and Cockers could appear in the same litters, the only breed difference being size. The Cocker, which is descended from the original spaniels of Spain, was first and foremost bred as a hunting dog, to find and flush woodcock. The dogs' powerful build is perfect for covering ground quickly and moving through dense bush to retrieve game. The Cocker is a willing working dog, obedient and agile, and delights in carrying things about, searching, and bustling around. Full of energy, it is naturally playful and affectionate, and loves being part of a family.

Appearance: The English Cocker Spaniel is a well balanced and compact breed. It has low-slung ears, long hair, and a gentle, relaxed expression.

Color: The Cocker can be found in a range of solid colors—black, liver, and shades of red—as well as black and tan, and liver and tan. It can also be parti-colored, with the solid color being broken by clearly marked, ticked, or roaned sections of white.

41. English Setter

Elegant and dignified, the English Setter is a descendant of the ancient family of sporting dogs. Bred from the fourteenth century, the English Setter was originally a trained bird dog, prized for its ability to work during the hunt rather than for its appearance. Believed to be a mix of Spanish Pointer, the large Water Spaniel, and the Springer Spaniel, the resultant combination is a fine hunting dog, known for its proficiency in seeking out and pointing game over expansive countryside. The modern Setter was refined through skilful breeding programs in the nineteenth century, and to this day this extremely devoted, good-natured, and friendly dog is equally at ease in the field and in the house. These are sweet, gentle, and loving dogs that enjoy family life and have an affinity with children.

Appearance: English Setters are of medium height, clean in outline, with a long, silky, flat coat. The sexes appear distinctly different: the male much more masculine in build, while the female has more refined features.

Color: The English Setter comes in a variety of colors including orange and white (orange belton), white with black markings (blue belton), tricolor (blue belton and tan), lemon belton, and liver belton.

42. English Springer Spaniel

The English Springer Spaniel's name derives from the breed's ability to flush birds rapidly, "springing" them into the air. This is considered the oldest of the spaniel breeds, and the forefather to all other land spaniels with the exception of the Clumber. Once grouped together with Cockers, and often found in the same litter, the Springer was finally classified as a separate breed in the late nineteenth century. The dogs are unmistakable members of the spaniel family, with their pendulous ears, gentle expression, sturdy build, and welcoming wagging tail. Every inch a sporting dog, the Springer is active and lively, combining beauty and intelligence, enthusiasm, and obedience. These dogs respond well to training and also love playing games, especially retrieving a ball.

Appearance: The English Springer Spaniel is a handsome breed—compact, solid, and symmetrical, with a docked tail. The breed has longer legs than the other British land spaniels, and the most streamlined build.

Color: Black or liver with white markings or the reverse, blue or liver roan, tricolor (black and white or liver and white with tan markings).

43. Flat-coated Retriever

The friendly, happy-go-lucky Flat-coated Retriever has the lightest build of all the retrievers. A mix of Irish Setter, Labrador, Water Dog, and Lesser Newfoundland, the Flat-coated Retriever's skills as a bird dog and swimmer meant it was much admired by English gamekeepers, who embraced the breed during the nineteenth century. Like many breeds, numbers of Flat-coated Retrievers decreased dramatically during the First and Second World Wars, and it is thanks to a few dedicated fanciers that we are able to enjoy these dogs today. They are affectionate and playful, with a well balanced and stable temperament and a puppy-like disposition. They love being around children, and their intelligent approach to life means they are also valuable guard dogs. Flat-coated Retrievers are quiet at home and lively outside, making them perfect family dogs.

Appearance: The Flat-coated Retriever is a medium-sized dog, but more slender and with a less square foreface than other retrievers. Its signature coat is dense and flat, and can shine brilliantly when well groomed.

Color: Black or liver.

44. German Shorthaired Pointer

Aristocratic and powerful, the German Shorthaired Pointer is an ideal all-purpose dog. The breed combines hunting skills with clean lines, elegant looks, and an agreeable temperament. During the nineteenth century German hunters desired a dog with a good nose and sound pointing ability. The dog needed to trail and retrieve from both water and land, with game including pheasant, quail, grouse, waterfowl, coons, possum, and even deer. It is believed that the breed's basic stock was the German Bird Dog, Old Spanish Pointer, and English Foxhound crossed with local German scent hounds (Schweisshunde). Eventually the English Pointer was introduced to the mix, resulting in a much faster and more energetic breed. A versatile and natural hunter, the German Shorthaired Pointer requires little training and is an ideal dog for the weekend hunter on foot. Their friendly, intelligent, and eager nature makes them well suited to family life, and they are most content when physically and mentally stimulated.

Appearance: A handsome, well balanced, medium-sized dog with a clean-cut head, long sloping shoulders, powerful back, and well-carried tail, all showing great power, endurance, and speed. Alert and energetic, its movements are well coordinated. The dog's muscular build is covered by a smooth, gleaming coat.

Color: Solid liver or a combination of liver and white (ticked, patched, or roan).

45. Golden Retriever

Friendly, responsible, and mild mannered, the Golden Retriever has become one of the most recognized, versatile, and popular breeds in history. It is a relatively young breed, developed in the mid-nineteenth century on the border between England and Scotland. The foundation for the breeding stock was the light-colored Tweed Water Spaniel, known for its intelligence, courage, and sporting ability. Later the blood of Irish Setter, Bloodhound, and more Tweed Water Spaniel was added, resulting in the Golden Retriever of today. Intelligent and easily trained, they were used primarily as hunters, although they also proved to be strong in the show ring. An all-around breed, Golden Retrievers are very adaptable, and they are widely used in many roles including as guide dogs for the blind, drug and explosives dogs, hunters, and companions. A devoted breed with a generous, loving nature, the Golden Retriever is a favored household dog and family pet with immense patience, making it particularly suited to families with children.

Appearance: The Golden Retriever is a powerful, medium-sized dog, well balanced, with a kindly expression. The head is broad, with pendulous ears. It is a solid dog, neither clumsy nor over-long in the leg. It has a dense, water-resistant undercoat, with a flat, wavy topcoat.

Color: Rich, radiant golden of various shades.

46. Gordon Setter

The Gordon Setter was originally developed in Scotland during the seventeenth century as a hunting dog. The breed increased in popularity when the Fourth Duke of Gordon became a passionate supporter in the nineteenth century. Its excellent sense of smell and proficiency at pointing and retrieving make the Gordon Setter a notable bird dog. Although not fast compared with other hunting dogs, it is an unparalleled one-person shooting dog due to its hunting ability on both water and land, keen intelligence, and retentive memory. The Gordon is considered the most conscientious and intelligent of the standing breeds, and with no need for repeated training they seem to improve with age. Alert, curious, and confident, even fearless, the Gordon is also friendly and eager to please. They respond well to training and enjoy an active lifestyle, and their obedient, sensible, and pleasant nature makes them loyal companions as well as reliable workers.

Appearance: The Gordon Setter is heavier than other setters, sturdily built and well muscled. It gives an impression of intelligence and dignity, with a finely chiseled head and strong, symmetrically balanced body. It has a level back, short tail, and a long, silky textured coat.

Color: Rich shining black with tan markings, presenting as either rich chestnut or mahogany.

47. Irish Setter

Full of fun and affection, mischievous, and intelligent, the Irish Setter is often referred to as having a "rollicking" personality. Bred as a gundog and used in the sport of falconry, the Irish Setter quickly proved its sporting ability. In the nineteenth century it became popular not only in its native Ireland but throughout the British Isles. Its lineage is generally accepted as being a mix of Irish Water Spaniel, Irish Terrier, English Setter, Spaniel, Pointer, and Gordon Setter. Originally the coat was red and white, and the solid red that is typical today was bred selectively during the early nineteenth century. Irish Setters are admired as reliable field companions, with a strong hunting instinct combined with an untiring eagerness. They are highly active, and their even temperament and sweet nature make them a highly enjoyable family member.

Appearance: The Irish Setter has an aristocratic and elegant appearance. It stands over 2 feet tall from the shoulder, and its signature red coat is glossy and straight. The coat is short and fine on the head and front of the legs, and sits longer on the back, chest, tail, and back of the legs.

Color: Mahogany or rich chestnut red. White can appear on the chest, throat, chin, or toes, or as a narrow-centred streak on the face.

48. Irish Water Spaniel

Intelligent and curious, the Irish Water Spaniel, like most sporting dogs, is an active, energetic, and willing companion. It is an ancient breed, with archaeological evidence of similar-type dogs from the seventh and eighth centuries. In the late twelfth century the breed was known as the Shannon Spaniel, Rat-tail Spaniel, or Whip-tail Spaniel. The beginnings of the modern Irish Water Spaniel developed from Ireland's Southern and Northern Water Spaniels during the 1800s. During this time Justin McCarthy is attributed with refining and fixing the breed type, and his famed "Boatswain" Irish Water Spaniel is often credited with being the first of the breed we know today. The breed quickly became popular as hunting dogs, and with their hardy weather-resistant coat, excellent swimming ability, and immense stamina they were well suited to the cold North Sea waters. Their clever, spirited nature and willingness to please make them great working dogs and easy-going companions.

Appearance: The Irish Water Spaniel is a well-designed gundog, with a strong and compact build. A picture of strength and endurance, they are easily identified by their topknot of long, loose curls, a dense and tightly curled coat, alongside a smooth face and rat-like tail.

Color: A rich dark liver, often appearing to have a purplish tint or bloom.

49. Labrador Retriever

The Labrador Retriever—also once known as the Black Water Dog, Lesser Newfoundland, or St. John's Water Dog—originated in Newfoundland, Canada. It is a descendant of the swimming dogs used to haul fishing nets to shore in the icy waters of Canada. Much admired for their hunting and swimming skills, these dogs were eventually taken to England in the early nineteenth century. Once there they faced a rocky future, and the breed nearly disappeared as a result of a heavy dog tax and quarantine laws. Restricted importation of the breed caused the remaining dogs to be crossed with other local breeds. Eventually the Labrador Retriever standard was fixed and recognized as a distinct breed by the English Kennel Club in 1903. Relaxed, eager to please, and intelligent, the Labrador Retriever has been enthusiastically embraced as a loving and playful family member. Well known for their willingness to learn and their dutiful manner, they are also highly valued guide and rescue dogs.

Appearance: The Labrador Retriever is a stocky, medium-sized dog, with an athletic and well balanced build. The distinctive coat is short, dense, and weather-resistant, with an "otter" tail. Friendly eyes are set in a broad head with a powerful jaw.

Color: Sought-after colors are solid black, yellow ranging from fox red to light cream, and shades of chocolate from light to dark.

50. Spinone Italiano

Also known as the Italian Spinone, Italian Coarse-haired Pointer, Italian Pointer, or Italian Griffon, the Spinone Italiano is loyal and gentle, while also a rugged and hardworking hunting dog. Like all European hunting breeds the Spinone was bred for the local landscape and climate: in this case the mountains, marshes, and dense forests of northwest Italy. Although the details are undocumented, the breed is believed to be a mix of Coarse-haired Italian Setter, White Mastiff, and possibly French Griffon. This versatile gundog has a long history of service to humans, and is highly regarded for its keen sense of smell and soft bite. With an untiring attitude to work, the Spinone is dedicated to fulfilling its owner's commands. The dogs are also very sociable, courageous, and affectionate, with the result that today they are becoming sought-after pets. Their intelligent, independent yet easygoing nature makes them playful and devoted companions for life.

Appearance: The Spinone Italiano is a powerful and muscular dog that shows great energy and strength. Solid and square-built, they have a thick, slightly wiry coat that is ideal for all weather conditions.

Color: Solid white, white with orange markings, orange roan with or without orange markings, white with brown markings, brown roan with or without brown markings.

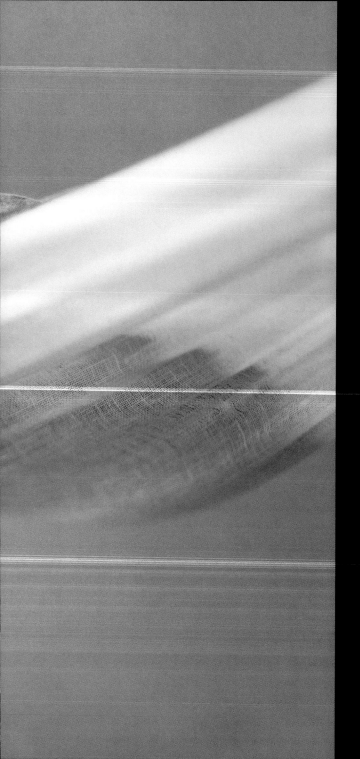

51. Vizsla

The Vizsla, also known as the Hungarian Vizsla or Hungarian Pointer, is a medium-sized dog and a natural hunter. The breed is of ancient origin, and these dogs are believed to have roamed Central Europe over a thousand years ago, following their Magyar masters and settling in what is now Hungary. Long favored by the aristocracy, they are recorded in etchings dating from the tenth century and literature from the fourteenth century. The Vizsla combines the fine hunting skills of the pointer and the retriever, resulting in an all-around working dog. Fast and steady, with an excellent nose, it works exceptionally well in open ground or in thick cover. This noble breed was threatened with extinction during the First and Second World Wars, until it was smuggled out of Hungary, ensuring our continued enjoyment of this gentle, sensitive, yet fearless dog. Lively and intelligent, with a friendly disposition and an instinctively protective nature, the Vizsla is a superior hunting dog that makes a worthy companion at home or in the field.

Appearance: Solid though lightly built, the Vizsla has a well-muscled body with a noble head, keen eyes, and an intelligent and alert expression.

Color: Solid golden rust in different shadings.

52. Weimaraner

The handsome and athletic Weimaraner is considered to be a young breed, dating only from the early nineteenth century. Bred with speed, scenting ability, courage, and intelligence in mind, the Weimaraner was developed at the court of the Grand Duke Karl August of Weimar. He specifically wanted an all-around hunting dog capable of tracking the wolves, wildcats, and deer that were abundant in Germany at that time. Once the breed was perfected its secrets were well guarded, and the dogs were only allowed to be owned by nobility. This history of exclusivity carried forth into the first Weimaraner Club of Germany, established in 1896, as one could only acquire a Weimaraner if membership of the club was obtained first. Alert, intelligent, and active, Weimaraners thrive on physical and mental stimulation. They are affectionate and friendly toward those they know, but will act as a formidable guard when their family is threatened.

Appearance: The breed's characteristic gray coat is reflected in its nickname, the "gray ghost." Bred for speed and endurance, the dogs are of medium size with long racing legs. They have a handsome face with a strong jaw and distinctive shaded blue or amber eyes. Their coats are commonly short, smooth, and sleek, although there is a rarer long-haired variety.

Color: Solid shades of mouse-gray to silver-gray.

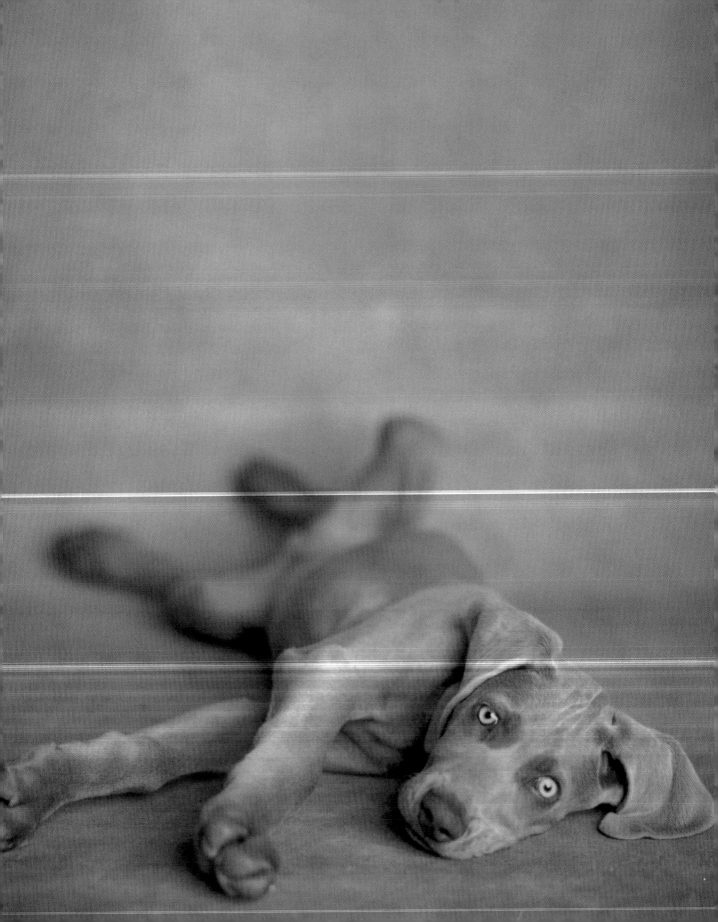

Nonsporting

53. American Bulldog

A hardy, athletic, and confident dog, the American Bulldog is taller, more agile, and swifter then its English counterpart. Although it is descended from the English Bulldog, the latter has been bred out to the more modern, softer breed we know today, while the original Bulldog was preserved in the American South. Longer in the leg than the English Bulldog, with a powerful, athletic body, the dogs were used to hunt wild boar, squirrel, and raccoon, as well as being trained as drivers and guardians of farming stock. Admired for their strength, intelligence, and devotion, American Bulldogs are known for heroic acts of courage when protecting their owners. They are a gentle, caring breed, protective and loving with children, and a loyal family dog.

Appearance: The American Bulldog has a muscular, sturdy body yet remains agile and light on its feet. A large, strong, square head and box-shaped muzzle support a powerful jaw. The coat is short, tight, and stiff to the touch.

Colors: All white, pied, brindle, or with red patches.

54. Bichon Frise

Originating in the Mediterranean area, the Barbichon, or Bichon, was used as a form of currency by early sailors, and brought to the Canary Island of Tenerife by the Spanish (alternative names are Bichon Tenerife and Tenerife Dog). Small, playful yet gentle, the Bichon were great traveling companions. With their powder-puff look and merry disposition, they became favored by the Italians during the fourteenth century, and by the nobility during the French Renaissance. Their fame reached its height during the reign of Henry III and Napoleon III, but their popularity declined in the late nineteenth century and led to less glamorous roles, such as accompanying organ-grinders and as part of the circus. It was not until 1933 that the official breed standard was registered, in France, and it was finally named "Bichon Frise" ("frise" being the French for curly, or curly-haired). Well known for its cheerful nature, the Bichon is at home with people of all ages. They love to play and tend to be good with children, making them a great family dog.

Appearance: The Bichon is small and pretty, with a solid body. The Bichon has an alert look, and dark, inquisitive eyes that reflect its playful temperament and sweet nature.

Color: White with possible subtle shadings of buff, cream, or apricot around the ears or on the body.

55. Boston Terrier

The Boston Terrier is an energetic and intelligent dog, fondly referred to as the American gentleman due to its sweet temperament. A native U.S. breed, it was developed by crossing two English dogs, the Bulldog and the white English Terrier. In 1889 a large group of fanciers located in the Boston area organized themselves into the American Bull Terrier Club and started showing the dogs. At the time they were known as Round Heads or Bull Terriers, but with increased opposition from Bull Terrier and Bulldog fanciers the club finally gave them the title Boston Terrier. Requiring little maintenance and exercise, over time the breed has increased in popularity as a family companion. They are admired for their gentle temperament and especially enjoy the company of children. Although lightweight they make excellent watchdogs, and their sharp, intelligent manner fits well into family life.

Appearance: The Boston Terrier is a well-balanced dog of medium size with a smooth coat, short head, compact body, and short tail. Wide-set, round eyes, and large prick ears enhance an alert and intelligent expression.

Color: The Boston Terrier usually appears as brindle, seal, or black with white markings, the most popular coat being brindle.

56. Chinese Shar-pei

Reserved and discerning with strangers, the Chinese Shar-pei is affectionate and loyal to its family. It is an ancient breed, believed to have originated in the area of Tai Li in the Chinese province of Kwantung. Statues strongly resembling the Shar-pei and manuscripts that mention "wrinkled dogs" help establish the breed's ancestry in the Han Dynasty (c. 200 BC). Following the prohibition of dogs during China's politically charged 1970s, the Shar-pei faced certain extinction until breeders in Hong Kong and Taiwan lobbied American fanciers to help save the breed. Today the unusual dog, with its wrinkled and rough sandpaper-like coat (reflected in the name, which means "sandy coat") and distinctive blue-black tongue, is extremely popular and in no danger of disappearing. A smart, dignified, and charming dog, with a regal and sober appearance, it has a calm and friendly nature and is unequivocally devoted to its family.

Appearance: The Shar-pei is a medium-sized dog with a square profile and a head that is slightly large for its body. As a puppy the short, harsh coat is loose and wrinkled over most of the body, but in the adult this looseness may be restricted to the head, neck, and withers. A "hippopotamus" muzzle and high-set tail are other distinctive features.

Color: The Shar-pei comes in a range of solid colors as well as brindle, spotted, and patterned.

57. Chow Chow

Known for its guarded and aloof response toward strangers, the Chow Chow is an intelligent, independent, and protective breed. Believed to be over 2,000 years old, the Chow originated in China and was developed for hunting, herding, and sled driving. A select few that were born smoky blue in color were promoted to the position of Buddhist temple dog. The name Chow Chow is believed to have evolved from the pidgin-English term meaning knick-knacks, a probable reference to the dog's position on trade ships during the nineteenth century. The breed's rise in popularity followed Queen Victoria's interest in the "wild dog of China," a title the Chow was given at the London Zoo. Today the breed is a fashionable pet and guard dog, admired for its loyalty and devotion to its owner.

Appearance: Strong, muscular, and heavy boned, the Chow is a sturdy and powerful dog. It has a compact body, with a plush rough double coat, and a tail set high. It carries itself with confidence, and has an unusual stilted gait. The head is large, with a broad, flat skull and short deep muzzle, with a blue-black tongue.

Color: The Chow comes in five colors: red, black, blue, cinnamon, and cream, and can appear clear colored, solid, or solid with lighter shadings in the ruff, tail, and featherings.

58. Dalmatian

The Dalmatian's history is shrouded in mystery, although a popular theory links the breed with its namesake country, Dalmatia. It is known that the breed has been unchanged for centuries, and has lived throughout numerous continents. Paintings on Egyptian royal tombs, letters dating from the mid-sixteenth century, and a fresco in the Spanish Chapel in Florence dated 1360 all depict a spotted dog. Similarly marked dogs also accompanied gypsies as they traveled from India through Europe and on to England. The breed served in various roles: from border sentinel in Dalmatia and Croatia to farm dog, sporting dog, performer, firedog, and coach dog. The Dalmatian is a very active dog, capable of great endurance and speed. At the same time it is poised and dignified, and their friendly, gentleman-like qualities make these dogs very easy to love. Sensible, faithful, and well mannered, they are devoted companions.

Appearance: The Dalmatian's distinctive spotted coat is short, fine, and dense, and appears sleek and glossy. It has a strong and muscular body, with a fairly long head.

Color: White base color, with spots of either black or liver covering the body from head to feet.

59. English Bulldog

The English Bulldog is a friendly and good-natured dog that gives an impression of strength and dignity. It is also a tenacious dog, and can appear stubborn. Initially developed in Britain as a ferocious dog with immense courage, suited to dogfighting and bullbaiting, the modern Bulldog retains none of its predecessor's fierce qualities. After these sports became illegal in England, dedicated breeders sought to retain only the desirable qualities of the breed. Today the Bulldog is considered one of the finest physical specimens of dog, and it is admired for its gentle nature and friendly manner. Kind and mellow, the Bulldog is good with children and strangers.

Appearance: The English Bulldog has a heavy, low-slung body of medium size, with wide shoulders and a massive short-faced head. The coat is short and smooth, highlighting the breed's muscular structure.

Color: The Bulldog comes in a range of solid colors and brindles, from red brindle through to all other brindles, solid white, solid red, fawn, or fallow, and piebald through to solid black.

60. French Bulldog

The French Bulldog is believed to be a descendant of the toy English Bulldog, which was brought to France around the middle of the nineteenth century during a time of increased migration. Once in France they were eventually crossed with various local breeds and given the name Boule-Dog Français. With time two varieties developed: one with "bat" ears and one with "rose" ears. The distinctive "bat" ears won the hearts of American fanciers, and the first organization in the world devoted to the breed was established in the United States. Today the breed's charming personality has earned it many loyal fans. The dogs are well behaved, affectionate, and playful, and make excellent family pets. Their patience, even disposition, and compact size also make them perfect companions for the elderly.

Appearance: The French Bulldog is a muscular, compact dog of medium or small stature. They are heavy boned, with short, smooth coats, and have an alert and inquisitive expression.

Color: The most popular colors are brindle, fawn, and white. A tidy central band down the forehead is prized.

61. Keeshond

The lively, intelligent Keeshond (pronounced Kayz-hawnd) is a member of the Spitz family, which originated in the Arctic or possibly sub-Arctic region. The Keeshond was greatly admired in Holland, and during the eighteenth century the breed became a political icon. Claimed as a symbol by the Patriots, who were led by Kees de Gyselare, the dogs fell into disfavor when the Prince of Orange obtained power and few people wanted to own a dog linked to the opposition. Their revival began in the 1920s, and gradually their popularity increased throughout Europe. The Keeshond is intelligent, friendly, and affectionate, loves human companionship, and enjoys the playful attention of children. Their alert nature and sharp hearing also means they make excellent watchdogs.

Appearance: Handsome and well balanced, the Keeshond has a squarish body covered by an abundant coat, lion-like mane, and a richly plumed tail that curves over the back. It has small pointed ears and an alert, fox-like expression.

Color: Dramatically marked, Keeshonds are a mixture of gray, black, and cream.

62. Lhasa Apso

The Lhasa Apso originated in the area surrounding the sacred city of Lhasa in Tibet, one of three non-sporting breeds native to this geographically harsh country. Originally called Abso Seng Kye, which translates as "Bark Lion Sentinel Dog," they were used primarily as guard dogs. Although their appearance seems at odds with this role, their sharp hearing and alert nature made them excellent watchdogs, guarding the inside of a dwelling while Mastiffs guarded the outside. The Lhasa Apso was considered to bring good luck, and traditionally they were never bought or sold but gifted to people. They eventually found their way around the world, and are believed to have been brought to America as a gift from the Dalai Lama. They tend to shy away from strangers, and loyally defend their home. Intelligent, happy, and devoted, Lhasa Apsos are today popular family pets.

Appearance: Well balanced and compact, the Lhasa Apso stands around the 1 foot mark at the withers. It is well adorned with a heavy, dense, and straight coat, with good fall over the eyes, good whiskers, and beard.

Color: Black, white, brown, golden, sandy, honey, dark grizzle, slate, smoke, or parti-color.

63. Lowchen

Although the Lowchen is recorded in literature and images dating from the mid-fifteenth century, the dog's origins are not clearly known. Initially thought to have originated in the Mediterranean, the Lowchen is now considered by many to be native to Germany (the name is German for "little lion"). The once-popular breed declined during the nineteenth century and following the Second World War they were named "rarest breed." A dedicated breeding program ensured the breed's survival, and it has once more gained in popularity. Alert and inquisitive, the "little lion" has traditionally been groomed to reflect its title, with close-cut hindquarters and a full, natural mane. The Lowchen is a loving and easily managed family pet—small, active, intelligent, and obedient.

Appearance: A stylish, proud-looking dog with a well balanced and stocky body, with a relatively short topskull and muzzle.

Color: The Lowchen can appear in any color or combination of colors.

64. Standard Poodle

An elegant breed with an air of distinction, the Standard Poodle is known for its intelligent and obedient nature. The oldest of the three Poodle varieties, it is believed to originate from Germany, although this is hotly debated by the French who regard the Poodle as their national dog. The Poodle is named for its well-known water retrieving ability, from the German "Pudel" or "Pudelin," which means to splash in the water. The characteristic clipping of the Poodle's coat was initially done to assist the dogs when swimming and protect their vital organs from the icy water. Today the Standard Poodle is a much-loved and admired breed. Playful and very active, they are dogs that love companionship and the freedom to run and swim.

Appearance: Carrying themselves proudly, this stylish breed is squarely built and well balanced. The Standard Poodle stands over 1¼ feet at the highest shoulder point, and is typically clipped in the traditional fashion of a "puppy, sporting, English saddle, or continental" clip.

Color: All solid colors, which may show varying shades of the same color, with contrasting eye-rims, nose, and lips.

65. Tibetan Spaniel

The early Tibetan Spaniels are believed to be the "little lion" dogs of the Tibetan monks. Great spiritual value was placed on them, and the dogs were often gifted back and forth between Tibet and neighboring Buddhist countries. This exchange led to a variety of characteristics in the same strain: for example, shorter muzzles were dominant along the Chinese borders, while the monasteries typically bred smaller dogs. Principally regarded as companion dogs and thought to bring good luck, Tibetan Spaniels were also celebrated watchdogs. Sitting high on the walls of a monastery, they used their exceptional eyesight, barking an alarm when anyone approached. Today loved and admired throughout the world, Tibetan Spaniels still have a love of high places where they can sit and watch the world go by. Their intelligent, accommodating, and cheerful nature, combined with their small size, makes them ideal companions and family pets.

Appearance: An attractive, well balanced, small dog that appears slightly longer in the body than in height. Its small head is carried proudly, and it has a longish, silky coat.

Color: All colors and mixtures of colors, with a golden red being most common.

66. Tibetan Terrier

The friendly and affectionate Tibetan Terrier is the third of the nonsporting breeds native to Tibet (along with the Tibetan Spaniel and the Lhasa Apso). An ancient breed that dates back almost 2,000 years, the Tibetan Terrier was considered a treasured gift that was able to bestow good fortune on its owner. As a result, the breed was kept pure, as people feared that introducing mixes would lead to bad luck. The dogs were also valued as family pets, and widely used to help herd and guard stock. They eventually found their way to England around 1920, when a Tibetan Terrier was given to a visiting physician as thanks for aiding a sick woman. Named "terrier" only for their size, not any other terrier traits, they quickly grew in popularity. Valued for their love of people, and their sociable and lively natures, Tibetan Terriers make delightful companion dogs. They are intelligent and sensitive, shy around strangers, but devoutly loyal to their family.

Appearance: The Tibetan Terrier is a medium-sized, squarely built dog with a muscular physique hidden under a profuse coat. Their unique foot construction (large, flat, and round, with thick, strong pads), thick protective coat, and hair that falls over the eyes and foreface reflect the extreme conditions in which the breed developed.

Color: Any color or combination of colors from white to black.

Terrier

67. Airedale Terrier

The sweet and dependable Airedale Terrier is the largest of the terrier breeds. Developed as a vermin hunter about a hundred years ago in the county of Yorkshire in England, the breed was variously known as the Working, Waterside, and Bingley Terrier, but was later named after the Valley of Aire in Yorkshire. Crossing the ancient Old English Terrier and the Otterhound, a keen-nosed dog that is a talented swimmer, produced a larger and stronger hunting terrier. With its excellent eyesight and hearing, great agility, and unfaltering loyalty, this was the first breed used for police duty in Germany and Great Britain. The Airedale was also a valued wartime dog, relied on as a dependable dispatch-bearer because of its ability to keep going even when wounded. Its intelligence, faithfulness, and determined obedience all make for a great watchdog and loyal companion.

Appearance: The largest breed of terrier, the Airedale stands as tall as 2 feet. A hardy and wiry coat covers a solid build, and the bearded face is a distinguishing feature of this very handsome breed.

Color: The Airedale has a black or dark grizzle saddle, with tan head, ears, and legs.

68. Australian Terrier

A fast, friendly, and sturdy little dog, the Australian Terrier is one of the smallest working terriers. It was first developed to be both helper and companion to the Australian settlers during the nineteenth century, managing rodents and snakes as well as tending to sheep and cattle. The Australian Terrier was the first Australian breed to be recognized and shown in Australia, and accepted officially in other countries, with a standard for the breed established by 1896. As befits their heritage as versatile workers, these dogs have excellent hearing and vision, they are excellent jumpers, and born diggers. They have a friendly and self-assured nature, and great affinity with children, the elderly, and the disabled. All in all, a celebrated breed for show, city, home, or farmland.

Appearance: The Australian Terrier is a small, sturdy, and medium-boned terrier, longer than it is tall, with pricked ears and docked tail. It has a harsh-textured outer coat, a distinctive ruff and apron, and a soft, silky topknot.

Color: Blue and tan, solid sandy, or solid red.

69. Border Terrier

Affectionate, sociable, and easily trained, the Border Terrier is a loving companion and a fine working farm dog. Originally bred to serve farmers in the Cheviot Hills near the border between England and Scotland, this small, sturdy dog eventually became a valued family dog. Fast and gutsy, the Border Terrier can stay abreast of a horse while still going to ground, making it an efficient hunter. Its role with the Border Hunt in Northumberland was acknowledged in 1870 when the name Border Terrier was adopted. The breed's love of company, cheerful nature, and good temper make the Border Terrier great to be around and an excellent family dog.

Appearance: The Border Terrier is a medium-sized dog with narrow shoulders and body. Lean and athletic, with a distinctive otter-like head, the Border Terrier is built to hunt and go to ground. It has a hard, wiry, weather-resistant outer coat and soft undercoat.

Color: The Border Terrier comes in a variety of colors from red, wheaten, grizzle, and tan to blue and tan.

70. Cairn Terrier

Spirited, bold, and inquisitive, the Cairn Terrier was developed as a working terrier in the Highlands of Scotland. It was particularly valued for its courage, agility, speed, and ability to scurry after the vermin inhabiting the rocky and wild terrain of the Isle of Skye. The modern Cairn has been carefully bred to retain these characteristics, and importance is placed on its height, which differs from other terriers. The Cairn delights in the company of people, and the dogs' engaging and affectionate disposition means they are excellent with children and make loving family members. They are known for their energetic and curious nature, epitomized by the most famous of the Cairn Terriers, Toto, in *The Wizard of Oz.*

Appearance: The Cairn has a well-proportioned body, not heavily built, with short legs. It stands well forward on its forelegs, and has strong hindquarters. A shaggy, weatherproof coat gives the dogs a somewhat fox-like appearance.

Color: The Cairn can range from cream through red or gray to almost black.

71. Irish Terrier

Playful and good tempered, the Irish Terrier was originally bred to eradicate vermin on Ireland's farmlands as well as to protect home and family. It is one of the oldest terrier breeds, whose popularity peaked in England in the late nineteenth century. The dogs' racy and hardy build, combined with an eagerness to please and hardworking temperament, made them ideal wartime messengers and sentinels. Still recognized as great hunting dogs, they have followed the path of numerous other breeds and successfully entered the home as family pets. They are instinctively loving and protective of those under their guard, and their affectionate and playful nature combined with a gentle tenderness makes them especially good with children.

Appearance: Character and appearance are highly valued by Irish Terrier breeders. The dog must be a picture of symmetry, proportion, and harmony, while being active and nimble in movement. Strong, with solid bone structure, they are built for power and endurance.

Color: "Whole-colored," with the most preferred colors being bright red, golden red, red wheaten, or wheaten. They can occasionally present with white on the chest. Irish Terriers sometimes have black hair as young puppies, which should disappear once they are fully grown.

72. Kerry Blue Terrier

Playful, lovable, and intelligent, the Kerry Blue Terrier takes its name from the mountainous region of County Kerry in Ireland. The breed is believed to have been developed by Ireland's peasantry to hunt the nobles' grounds in silence. They were used mainly for hunting small game and birds on land and water, as well as herding cattle and sheep. Their most distinguishing feature is their striking blue coat. Although they are born black, the coat slowly fades to a slate gray/bluish color by eighteen months. It was this handsome feature that influenced English fanciers to show the breed and raise its status from peasant hunting dog to stylish show dog. The Kerry Blue's gentle, friendly temperament and keen intelligence make it an extremely versatile working and sporting dog as well as a sociable and affectionate companion.

Appearance: Extremely proud, with the attitude of a champion, when groomed the tall, powerful Kerry Blue Terrier is one of the most striking of all dogs. Showing definite terrier style and character, the Kerry Blue is muscular and well balanced, with a characteristic soft, dense, and wavy coat.

Color: Any shade of tan or dark coloring appearing up to the age of eighteen months, then any shade of blue, with or without black points.

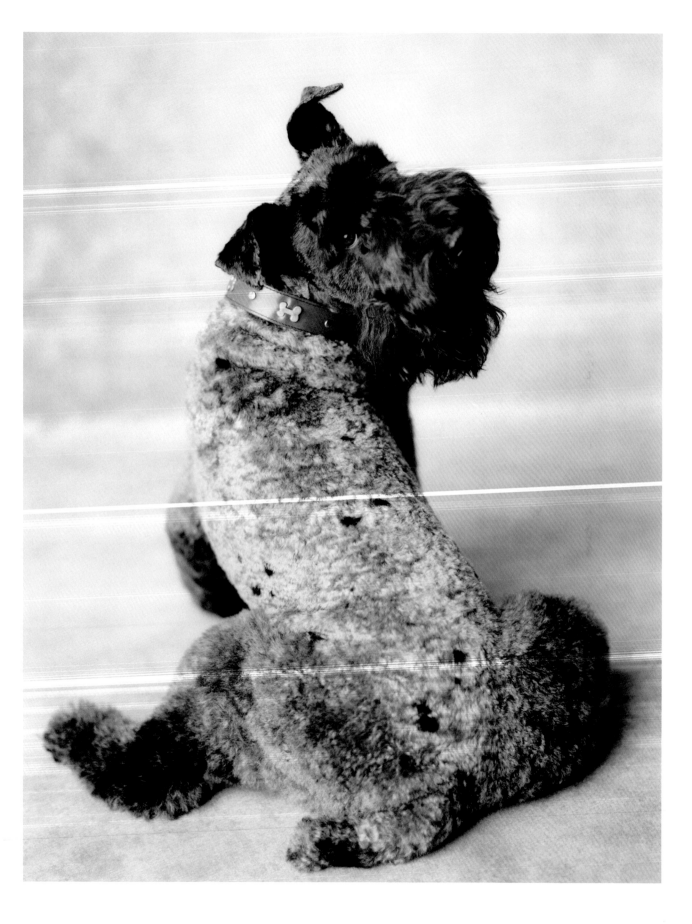

73. Miniature Schnauzer

The Miniature Schnauzer is a playful, inquisitive, and intelligent breed that originated in Germany. Resembling its larger cousin, the Standard Schnauzer, in everything but size, the Miniature is the most popular of the Schnauzer breeds. It was developed by crossing selectively small Standard Schnauzers with Affenpinschers and Poodles, and shown as a distinct breed from 1899. Used initially as farm dogs to keep the barn free of rats, their cheerful temperament and eagerness to please means they are also well suited to family life. They are known as the friendliest of the terrier dogs, and are happy in the company of children. Active and alert, like all terriers, the Miniature Schnauzer is a good watchdog, keen to signal a barking alarm when strangers approach.

Appearance: Powerfully built and robust, the Miniature Schnauzer appears almost square in shape: the length of its body is equal to the height of the shoulders. It has a distinctive harsh, wiry outer coat and a close soft undercoat, complemented by a luxurious whiskered beard and eyebrows.

Color: Most commonly seen in salt and pepper coloring, but can be black and silver or, less often, solid black.

74. Parson Russell Terrier

Specifically bred for fox hunting in the south of England during the nineteenth century, the Parson Russell Terrier is an adaptable and determined hunter. These dogs are known for their tireless drive and fearlessness, and the ability to follow the hounds over long distances, go to ground, and hold the fox at bay. The breed is named after the most famous of British huntsmen, the Reverend John Russell, known as "the sporting Parson." The Parson Russell is widely accepted as being a cross of the extinct Old English White Terrier and a black and tan terrier similar to the early Manchester. Intelligent, determined, and athletic, the Parson Russell is also very affectionate and friendly. It loves to play, and is at its best when mentally and physically stimulated.

Appearance: Built for speed and endurance, the Parson Russell Terrier is a well-balanced, medium-sized dog. Its harsh weatherproof coat, compact build, and small flexible chest are all signs of its initial role as a superior hunting dog.

Color: Predominantly white, but can be white with black or tan markings, or a combination of these colors. The colors should be clear.

75. Scottish Terrier

The Scottish Terrier was developed in Scotland during the eighteenth century to hunt foxes and badgers. Originally named the Aberdeen Terrier, after the Scottish town of the same name, it is one o five terrier breeds that originated in Scotland. Later i was given the nickname "little diehard," a reference to its feisty nature. Its small size allowed it easily to go to ground after the hunt, while its stocky build and determined attitude made it a strong and enduring worker. Surprisingly agile for such a short-legged breed, the Scottish Terrier is today more stylish companion than revered hunter. Dignified anc bold, the Scottish Terrier is always alert and spirited. Although fiercely competitive toward other dogs, it is friendly and affectionate in the company of humans.

Appearance: Solid and thick-set, with a heavy-bonec body that is well covered with a hard, wiry, weather-resistant coat. Its abundant beard, fairly large, pricked ears, and upright, pointed tail are defining features.

Color: Wheaten, black, or brindle of any color, with the black or brindle showing possible white or silver sprinklings throughout the coat.

6. Soft-coated Wheaten Terrier

Playful, intelligent, and sweet-tempered, the Soft-coated Wheaten Terrier is one of three large terriers that originated in Ireland. Developed as an all-around farm dog, it was used not just in the usual terrier role of managing vermin, but to herd stock and protect family and estate. Through natural selection, only the strongest and bravest developed, resulting in a very well-designed dog of medium size. It is a dependable working dog, with a steadiness of temperament combined with the typical alertness and intelligence of the terrier. Graceful and happy-go-lucky, Wheatens love people and delight in affection. With their strong sporting instincts, these intelligent and confident dogs make wonderful companions.

Appearance: The Soft-coated Wheaten Terrier is medium sized, strong, square in shape, and well built. The signature wheaten coat that sets the breed apart from other terriers falls in abundant wavy or loose curls and is soft and silky to the touch.

Color: Any shade of wheaten.

77. West Highland White Terrier

The legend of the West Highland White Terrier is that one of the breed with a reddish coat was mistakenly shot for a fox, and it was this event that led to the decision that only white coats, which could be seen easily, should be bred. Legend aside, the West Highland White Terrier originated in Poltalloch, Scotland, and is believed to have existed well over a century ago. Once known as the Roseneath Terrier or Poltalloch Terrier, in 1909 the name was changed to the West Highland White Terrier. Admired for their intelligent, cunning, and faithful hunting style when on the field, when off duty they are playful, good natured, and considered by many to be the friendliest of terriers. Always curious with an outgoing personality, they love people and attention. On occasion they have been described as "a lot of Scottish spunk in a small body."

Appearance: Hardy looking, though not stocky like the Scottish Terrier, the West Highland White Terrier is well balanced, with a straight back and powerful legs. The harsh, straight coat is generally left longer on the back and sides, while trimmed to blend into the shorter coat on the neck and shoulders.

Color: Pure white.

Toy

78. Brussels Griffon

Intelligent, alert, sensitive, and proud, the Brussels Griffon is a robust member of the toy group. Although there is little record of the Griffon's development, it is accepted that nineteenth-century coachmen kept small terrier types for managing stable rats—these dogs were Affenpinscher-like, known as Griffons d'Ecurier or wire-coated stable dogs, and were descendants of the German Affenpinscher and the Belgian street dog. Strains of Pug, King Charles Spaniel, and Ruby Spaniel were later introduced. This resulted in two distinct varieties, one smooth-coated and one with a rough, bewhiskered coat. The strong facial features that characterize the Brussels Griffon are largely the result of the spaniel strain. As the need for stable dogs diminished, these sensitive dogs eventually found their way into homes as valued companions and family dogs. The breed acquired fame when a Brussels Griffon played a leading role alongside Jack Nicholson in the 1997 hit film *As Good As It Gets*.

Appearance: The Brussels Griffon's distinctive face— which has an almost human expression—is short, upturned, large, and round, with a short nose and unusually large, prominent black eyes. It has a short, sturdy, thickset body, with either of two coat types: rough or smooth.

Color: The Brussels Griffon comes in a variety of colors, including a rich red, beige, black and tan, and all black, with occasional white spots or blaze on any colored coat.

79. Cavalier King Charles Spaniel

The Cavalier King Charles Spaniel is a delightfully affectionate, playful, and intelligent dog. Once a luxury item, recorded on tapestries and paintings for centuries alongside their aristocratic families, the breed was named after King Charles II of Britain who was a passionate admirer of the dog. When his reign ended, the breed was discarded and almost became extinct. Queen Victoria reinstated the honor of the Cavalier, but by then the breed had changed dramatically from the original. The Cavalier we know today has been carefully modeled on its royal forebears, and following a revitalized breeding program it was classified as a separate breed in the 1940s. The Cavalier King Charles is an ideal house pet, with a happy, outgoing, and loving temperament. These dogs love to explore and play, but their intelligence and eagerness to please means that they respond well to training.

Appearance: The Cavalier is a small, well-balanced, moderately boned dog with a medium-sized chest and shoulders well set back. The coat is long and silky.

Color: Ruby (red), black and tan, Blenheim (a rich chestnut and white mix), and tricolor (black, white, and tan).

80. Chihuahua

The tiny Chihuahua is an extremely lively, enterprising, and proud breed that was once considered to be sacred. Considered the oldest dog on the North American continent, the breed is named after the Mexican state of Chihuahua. It is believed to be descended from the Techichi, a small companion dog of the ancient Toltecs, who lived in what is now Mexico as early as the ninth century. Images have been found of dogs similar to the Chihuahua on the pyramids of Cholula and the ruins of Chicen Itza on the Yucatan Peninsula. It is believed this breed was crossed with the Chinese Crested to produce the modern day, smaller Chihuahua. Today the Chihuahua is a popular companion dog, equally giving of attention as demanding of it. In temperament it has some of the characteristics of a terrier, and is intelligent, although slightly stubborn. An extremely loyal dog, it can be trained well with patience.

Appearance: The Chihuahua is a small, well-proportioned, and dainty dog. There are two varieties: smooth-coated and long-coated. The Chihuahua has large, erect ears, and round eyes set wide.

Color: The Chihuahua comes in a variety of colors, including red, white, chocolate, and black, although the most recognized color is fawn.

81. Chinese Crested

The Chinese Crested is a friendly, playful, and intelligent dog. There are two varieties: the Hairless and the Powder-puff. They are believed to be descended from the African hairless dog, which was widely dispersed throughout the world by merchant traders. Admired for their small size, they were eventually bred even smaller by the Chinese and further traded throughout Central and South America, Asia, and Africa. Europe seemingly fell in love with the breed during the nineteenth century, when they were depicted in art and architecture. The Chinese Crested loves to dig and climb, and they were formerly used as hunters of small vermin. These dogs crave human affection and hugs, and they enjoy the company of children. They can also be trained to perform tricks.

Appearance: The Chinese Crested is a toy dog that is small, active, and fine boned. The Hairless has hair only on the head, feet, and tail. The Powder-puff, which is heavier in build, is completely covered with fur.

Color: The Chinese Crested can appear in a variety of colors, with the most common a white to silvery white.

82. Havanese

The Havanese is an old breed that originated in the Mediterranean. It is believed Spanish traders took these small dogs to Cuba in the early sixteenth century. Much admired by the Cuban aristocracy, the Havanese developed independent of outside influence and produced their unique coat texture in isolation. By the mid-eighteenth century their fame had grown, and they became popular pets of the European elite. The breed has remained virtually unchanged during the past 150 years. Eleven Havanese found their way to the United States during the Cuban revolution, and it is acknowledged that the modern breed derives from these select few. Their eagerness to please and gentle nature makes them a charming and much-admired family dog. They are devoted animals, affectionate, sweet-tempered, and loyal. They are also intelligent and respond well to training.

Appearance: A small, sturdy dog, the Havanese is slightly longer than it is tall. It is covered with abundant long, silky, wavy hair.

Color: The Havanese appears rarely in pure white and is more common in different shades of fawn from light fawn to havana brown (a reddish-brown tobacco color).

83. Maltese

Gentle yet playful, the Maltese is a dog of great refinement and significant antiquity, well-documented for more than twenty-eight centuries. Venerated as an object of great beauty, the Maltese features in tributes scattered through ancient literature and paintings, and there are even Greek tombs dedicated to the little dog. An ancient Maltese statue discovered in Egypt further supports their honored place in society, where they were primarily owned by royalty and members of the aristocracy. The crusaders are believed to have introduced the breed to England, where they soon became popular companion dogs. They were first exhibited in America in 1877, and today are still adored as house pets and sought-after show dogs. Maltese are well known for their sweet and gentle temperament, although they also have considerable courage. Lively and playful, they are a joy to have around and take enormous pleasure from loyal and affectionate human company.

Appearance: Standing up to 10 inches tall, the Maltese is covered from head to foot with a long, silky coat. It has dark eyes and black eye-rims, which contrast beautifully with the whiteness of its full coat.

Color: Pure white with possible lemon or tan shading on the ears.

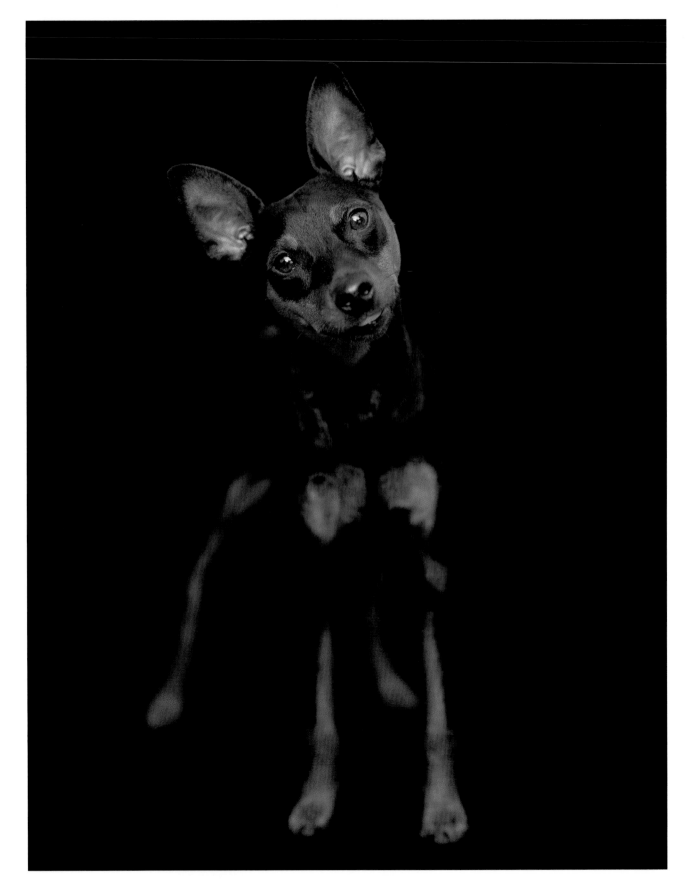

84. Miniature Pinscher

The Miniature Pinscher, referred to by fanciers as the "Min Pin," is an intelligent and spirited dog. Like many breeds, its history is hotly debated, with the earliest documentation dating from about 200 years ago. It is now widely accepted that the Min Pin is much older than this, and it has been linked to images in old artifacts and paintings. A breed native to Germany, researchers estimate that it is a mix of Dachshund, Italian Greyhound, and the shorthaired German Pinscher. The Min Pin is well known as a brave little watchdog, and is often referred to as "a big dog in a little body." Playful, full of energy, and always on the alert, the Min Pin makes a delightful companion.

Appearance: The Miniature Pinscher is sturdy in body yet very agile. Standing up to 1 foot high at the withers, it appears structurally well balanced and athletic. The coat is hard, short, and smooth.

Color: Solid red or stag red (red with an intermingling of black hair), blue, black, and chocolate all appear, with rust-red markings on the cheeks, lips, lower jaw, throat, above the eyes, the chest, lower forelegs, inside of hind legs and vent region, lower portion of hocks, and feet. Toes have black or brown penciling.

85. Papillon

The elegant and glamorous Papillon has been portrayed in paintings since the sixteenth century. The name *Papillon*—from the French word for butterfly—reflects the breed's distinctive appearance. A neat white strip down the centre of the face and nose highlights the large, erect ears, giving the combined effect of a butterfly. Although it owes its name and development to the French, it was the Spanish and Italians who fell in love with the breed and popularized it. It is an intelligent breed, obedient and responsive, easy to train, and capable of performing tricks. Friendly, happy, and alert, the Papillon enjoys human companionship and thrives on mental stimulation.

Appearance: The Papillon presents a picture of daintiness and elegance, with an attractive head and fine bone structure. A drop-eared variety is known throughout Europe as the Phalene (from the French word for moth). Both types have abundant straight, long-flowing, silky coats over surprisingly strong bodies.

Color: White with patches of a variety of colors except liver.

86. Pekingese

The legend of the Pekingese tells of a lion that asked the patron saint of animals, Ah Chu, to shrink him in size while keeping his great lion heart and character, so that he could finally wed his true love, the marmoset. The offspring of this magic union are said to be the dogs of Fu Lin, or the Lion Dog, which we now call Pekingese. The dogs were owned by Chinese royalty, and they are sometimes referred to as the "Sleeve Dog," a direct reference to their being carried in the voluminous sleeves of the Imperial House. Their documented history begins at the time of the Tang Dynasty, in the eighth century. However, the West only came to know the Pekingese in 1860 following a British raid on the Imperial Palace in which five Pekingese dogs were discovered (all others having been ordered to be killed so they would not fall into enemy hands). These five dogs are considered to be the forefathers of today's Pekingese. From a long history of luxurious worship, the Pekingese can be slightly stubborn and opinionated. At the same time they are affectionate and loyal, and this, combined with a suspicion of strangers, makes them worthy watchdogs.

Appearance: Small and well balanced, the Pekingese paints a picture of lion-like dignity and quality. It has a long, harsh-textured, and profuse coat that also forms a mane.

Color: The coat can appear in any color or marking except albino or liver.

87. Pomeranian

The Pomeranian is an animated dog whose cheerful temperament and small size appeals greatly to many people. Thought to be descended from the Icelandic sled dog, a member of the Spitz family, the Pomeranian is believed to have been bred down in size in the Prussian region of Pomerania. In the late nineteenth century, Queen Victoria fell in love with the breed and established her own Pomeranian kennels. In fact, her passion for the breed can be seen in depictions of her death bed, where she had a Pomeranian lying beside her. The breed's fame grew as a result of Queen Victoria's love of the dogs, and they remain much loved today. Its intelligent and inquisitive nature, combined with a love of attention, makes the Pomeranian an immensely enjoyable companion as well as a skillful show dog.

Appearance: The Pomeranian is compact and short backed, but very sturdy. The Pomeranian has an abundant harsh-textured coat with a heavily plumed tail set high and flat. Its expression is one of intelligence and alertness.

Color: The most common colorings are orange, black, or cream through to white.

88. Pug

A dog of considerable antiquity, the Pug is believed to have been a true breed since before 400 BC. Although probably named in reference to its facial expression, which was similar to the marmoset monkeys called Pugs, the breed has had an auspicious history. Pugs were first companions of the Buddhist monks in Tibet, and later a favorite pet in various royal courts throughout Europe and Asia. The breed was brought to England by King William II, after a Pug saved his life in 1572 when he was a young Prince of Orange. The dogs became fashionable accessories, and their popularity increased again after the British raid on the Chinese Imperial Palace in 1860, when the Pug, like the Pekingese, was again brought to England. Often described as "multum in parvo," meaning "a lot of dog in a small space," the Pug's outgoing and loving temperament warms hearts and makes it a favorite household pet. Known for its good nature and playfulness, it also has great affinity with children.

Appearance: The Pug has a squarely built body, strong legs, and a short, glossy coat. Its tightly curled tail provides a perfect balance for its distinctively squashed face, with its deep wrinkles. Its eyes are large and lustrous.

Color: Silver, apricot, fawn, or black.

89. Shih Tzu

The aristocratic, self-assured Shih Tzu (meaning lion) is descended from the smallest of the Tibetan holy dogs. Believed to have been bred in the Forbidden City of Peking, the Shih Tzu is depicted in paintings and objects dating from as early as AD 624, when a pair was reportedly gifted to the Chinese court. A beloved house pet of the Ming Dynasty (1368–1644), the breed nearly disappeared following the Communist Revolution, and today's Shih Tzu can be linked directly to the fourteen that survived. Shih Tzu carry themselves proudly and with great confidence, reflecting their early links with royalty. They are affectionate and bouncy dogs, and make delightful companions and loving family pets.

Appearance: The Shih Tzu presents a fine picture of aristocracy, with its head well up and tail set high and curved on the back. It is sometimes called the "chrysanthemum dog" because the hair on its face grows in all directions. A long dense coat covers a small but sturdy body.

Color: All colors, but a white blaze on the forehead and a white-tipped tail are highly prized.

90. Toy Poodle

The three Poodle varieties—Standard, Miniature, and Toy—are actually one breed governed by the same standard, but differing in size. Toy Poodles are considered to have the highest intelligence of the three, and are well known for their excellent learning abilities. Like the Standard Poodle, they are also capable swimmers. Although they originated in Germany, Poodles were most popular in France and reached enormous heights of fame during the reign of Louis XVI and Queen Anne, when the breed was a court favorite. It was in the twentieth century that the breed truly developed, however, and by the 1950s the Toy Poodle was securely established and officially given a separate status. Because of their small size and affectionate nature, Toy Poodles are very popular household pets. Devoted and loving, they make wonderful companion dogs.

Appearance: The Toy Poodle is an exact replica of the larger Standard Poodle. Squarely built and well balanced, it carries itself proudly. Where the Standard Poodle is over 1¼ feet at the highest point of the shoulders, and the Miniature Poodle is over 10 inches and up to 1¼ feet , the Toy Poodle is 10 inches or under.

Color: All solid colors, which may have varying shades of the same color, with contrasting eye-rims, nose, and lips.

91. Yorkshire Terrier

Although they became a fashionable women's accessory in the late Victorian era, the Yorkshire Terrier was originally developed by working-class Scotsmen who travelled to Yorkshire in search of factory employment on the weaving looms. Their lineage is linked to the now-extinct Waterside Terrier, a small dog with a longish coat that was a mix of Black and Tan English Terrier and the Paisley and Clydesdale Terriers. Initially Yorkshire Terriers were much bigger than the modern variety, and they were originally known as "broken-haired Scotch Terriers." Selective breeding miniaturized the breed, and they were renamed in 1870 after the Westmoreland Show, where it was reported they should "no longer be called Scotch Terriers but Yorkshire for having been so improved there." Their confident manner and luxurious coat make them a picture-perfect show dog when highly groomed. Definitely a terrier in nature, they are spirited and engaging. Affectionate with those they know, they love the rough and tumble of play with children.

Appearance: The Yorkshire Terrier's signature long coat hangs quite straight and parts evenly across the body and down the face. The body is compact and well proportioned, and the dogs display a self-assured manner.

Color: Pure dark steel-blue (not silver blue) with the hair on the chest a rich tan, darker at the roots and shading to a lighter tan at the tips.

Miscellaneous

92. Cavoodle

Originating in Australia, the Cavoodle is a cross of pure Miniature or Toy Poodle with the Cavalier King Charles Spaniel, producing a smaller version of the Cockapoo or Spoodle. The affectionate and sweet disposition of the Cavalier King Charles beautifully complements the Toy Poodle's qualities of extreme intelligence and loyalty. Bred as companion dogs, the Cavalier's laid-back and sociable qualities combined with those of the easily trained and responsive Poodle make the Cavoodle exceptionally well suited to family life. The cross has also seen the development of a healthier breed, with many of the genetic problems of the original breeds being greatly reduced. Easy to care for and extremely tolerant and gentle with children, these modern dogs are growing in popularity.

Appearance: The small, well-balanced, and moderately boned Cavoodle can appear in two varieties, either showing a Poodle-like coat or a soft and wavy Cavalier-like coat.

Color: Cavoodles may be white, caramel, apricot, black and white, and black and tan.

93. Dogue de Bordeaux

Theories abound about the true development of the Dogue de Bordeaux. Some believe they are descendants of the Tibetan Mastiff, while others believe they are possibly a cousin of the Neapolitan Mastiff. The Bullmastiff and the Bulldog are also considered by many to play a large part in the history of the Dogue. What is agreed, however, is that the Dogue is an ancient French breed. Used as guardian, hunter, and fighter, the Dogue was trained to bait bulls, bears, and jaguars, hunt boars, herd cattle, and protect homes. Twice in the breed's history they nearly fell into extinction: first during the French Revolution, when the dogs were killed alongside their wealthy masters, and again when Adolf Hitler demanded their destruction due to the extreme loyalty they showed to their owners. Today the Dogue de Bordeaux is regarded as a loving and loyal family member, extremely affectionate with children. Wary of strangers, they excel as guard dogs and protectors.

Appearance: The Dogue de Bordeaux is a powerful dog with a strong, athletic build. Muscular and sitting rather close to the ground, it appears stocky and imposing. It has a fine, short coat that is soft to the touch.

Color: All shades of fawn from a mahogany fawn to a light fawn, with a red, brown, or black mask.

94. Goldendoodle

The Goldendoodle is a loving and loyal breed that is believed to have originated in North America during the 1990s. Taking its name from its mixed heritage of Golden Retriever and Poodle, the Goldendoodle was bred as a larger version of the increasingly popular Cavoodle. It is greatly admired for the mixture of qualities it brings from both parent breeds. Goldendoodles have an affectionate and playful temperament, and their low-shedding coats make them ideal companions for allergy sufferers as well as perfect family pets. Goldendoodles are clever and easily trained, and tend to retain the strong retrieving instincts of the Golden Retriever. Sociable and even-tempered, they are known for their devotion to those under their care, and are tender and doting with children.

Appearance: Goldendoodles can vary greatly depending on the genetic pool of the parents, and differences can appear within a single litter. Typically they are grouped as standard or mini, reflecting crossbreeding with either a Standard or a Miniature Poodle. Their coats may be curly, wavy, or straight.

Color: White, blond, tan, chocolate, red, black, silver, parti, phantom, or a mix.

95. Japanese Spitz

Although small in stature, the Japanese Spitz is large in courage and vigor. Theories regarding the history of the breed abound, with many believing them to be a miniature version of the Samoyed dog, the companion breed of the nomadic tribes of Mongolia. Another theory connects them to the American Eskimo Dog. It is commonly believed that they traveled across Europe into Asia, and settled in Japan around AD 500. A playful, affectionate, and obedient dog, the breed was first developed by the Japanese as a home companion. While they are happy in the company of other pets, they particularly enjoy playing with children. They are alert and intelligent, and their protective attitude toward their family is reflected in a strong tendency to bark a warning when strangers approach, meaning they are also appreciated as bold watchdogs.

Appearance: A small breed, the Japanese Spitz has a broad, deep chest and appears strong and confident. It has a sharply pointed muzzle and triangular ears standing erect, with a bushy tail carried over the back. A beautiful dog, predominantly covered by a long, straight outer coat combined with a profuse short, dense, and soft undercoat.

Color: Pure white.

96. Kangal Dog

The powerful Kangal Dog originated in the Kangal District of Sivas Province in Central Turkey. It is believed to be related to the early Mastiff type depicted in Assyrian art, and was probably bred by the sultans of Turkey from the seventeenth century. Later they were developed by villagers to guard their flocks against large predators such as wolves, bears, and jackals. They were greatly admired for their immense strength, speed, and courage, and the breed has changed little since that time. Kangal Dogs are considered the national dog of Turkey, appearing on postage stamps and bred by government and national institutions. Relying on their formidable size to scare off any threat, they are not confrontational and are in fact extremely affectionate and loving dogs. Their protective instinct makes them incredibly loyal and sensitive to their owners, and they are especially patient and protective with children under their care.

Appearance: The Mastiff-like Kangal Dog is large and powerful, heavy-boned, with a massive head and a short, dense coat. The tail is typically curled.

Color: Solid color from a light dun or pale, dull gold to a steel gray, with possible white patches on the chest, feet, and chin, with a black mask.

97. Labradoodle

The intelligent and cheerful Labradoodle was developed in Australia during the 1970s following an inquiry from an allergy sufferer who needed a guide dog. As its name suggests, the breed is a cross between a Labrador and a Poodle. The Labrador was selected as a proven guide and rescue dog due to its gentle manner and high intelligence, while the Poodle is also extremely intelligent and has the quality of being nonshedding. Although still an extremely young breed, Labradoodles have won many hearts. Their nonshedding coats make them ideal for allergy sufferers, while their intelligence, versatility, and sociable natures make them perfect dogs for assistance/therapy work, seizure alert, and guide/companions. An all-around dog, they are easily trained and their friendly, playful nature makes them highly sought after as family pets.

Appearance: The Labradoodle is an athletic, medium-sized dog that can appear with either a wavy, free-flowing coat or a curling coat. Energetic yet graceful when free, Labradoodles are quiet and responsive when controlled.

Color: A variety of colors from silver, cream, and chocolate to a mix of reds.

98. Leonberger

The Leonberger has an intriguing history, essentially being bred as a marketing tool. In the nineteenth century, Heinrich Essig, a town councillor of Leonberg, Germany, set about developing a dog that looked like the lion that appeared on the town's coat of arms. The breed is a mix of Landseer Newfoundland, Saint Bernard, and Pyrenean Mountain Dog, with later mixes that have not been identified. Essig used the Leonberger to promote his town, donating the dogs to royalty—the Prince of Wales, King Umberto of Italy, the Tsar of Russia, and the Austrian Empress Elisabeth all owned Leonbergers. After Essig's death in 1889 the first Leonberger club was established, and by 1895 a standard was set. The standard was revised during a revamped breeding program following the Second World War, when the Leonberger was all but lost. Admired greatly for their intelligence and willingness to please, they are highly trainable to the point of following orders to jump out of helicopters. A patient and affectionate breed, they are often referred to as "nanny" dogs because of their affinity for children.

Appearance: Powerful and muscular, the Leonberger is slightly longer than tall, with a deep chest, and unusual webbed feet. It appears confident, moving with a strong, firm gait, and with a warm expression.

Color: Yellow, sandy, red to reddish brown, often with a black mask and markings.

99. Pyrenean Shepherd

An ancient breed, spoken of in some tales as evolving from the native Pyrenean bears and foxes, and as the original herding and hunting dog of the Cro-Magnon people in the Pyrenees. Accepted accounts of dogs as drovers and companions are well known in the French Pyrenees, dating from medieval times. Two types of field dog were used in the area, working side by side: the Great Pyrenees guard dog and the Pyrenean Shepherd drover. Working alongside the larger guarding dogs the Pyrenean Shepherds were able to retain their smaller size, which enabled them to be swifter and more agile. During World War I many Pyrenean Shepherds gave their lives as couriers and search and rescue dogs, and they became well known for their intelligence, speed, and courage. A hard-working dog, the Pyrenean Shepherd loves being in the field herding. They are extremely loyal and sensitive animals, and are highly affectionate and protective toward their family.

Appearance: A well-developed athlete, the Pyrenean Shepherd is small, lean, light-boned, and built as a horizontal rectangle. Full of energy and ready to be worked, the breed has great vivacity of movement, giving them a characteristic gait.

Color: Various shades of fawn and gray, merles of diverse tones, brindle, and black.

100. Spoodle

A hybrid breed, the Spoodle (also known as the Cockapoo, particularly in the United States) has been developed informally for nearly half a century, making it rather old in the modern designer-dog world. It is a cross of pure Cocker Spaniel and Poodle, and combines the Poodle's high intelligence and nonshedding coat with the Spaniel's sturdy build and sweet and patient nature. The resulting dogs are particularly sociable and openly affectionate. They are eager to please, and being extremely clever they respond very well to being trained. They have a great affinity with people and their forgiving nature makes them especially good with children.

Appearance: Squarely built and well balanced, the Spoodle is capable of great speed, agility and stamina. Depending on the parents they can vary in height from toy to miniature or standard, but all carry a large, round head with well-spaced eyes that have an alert and intelligent expression.

Color: Any solid color, parti-color, phantom (brown, black, or silver with contrasting areas), sable, brindle, or roan.

101. Dalmatian Boxer Cross

Kizzie, the 101st dog in this book, is my dog. She's a crossbred rather than a purebred but she couldn't be more special.

My love affair with canines began with our family dog, Archie, a nutty English Springer Spaniel. My family was new to dogs and we had no idea about training; Archie was very badly behaved, but we loved him. But it was a dog living around the corner from us as I was growing up that sparked my love for the affectionate and personable Newfoundland breed. As soon as I was old enough I bought my own Newfoundland, Henry, the love of my life. Henry went everywhere with me. He accompanied me on most of my photo shoots, and starred, uncomplainingly, in several of them. Henry was a huge inspiration for me and my work. Losing him left an unfathomable hole in my life.

It was two and a half years before I felt able to get another dog. A friend called to tell me she knew of a dog that needed to be rehoused. Suddenly the time was right, and I said yes before I even knew any details. I believe it was fate as Kizzie is the perfect companion for me. She came from a farm but has adapted brilliantly to city life, and we both get out and about in the countryside a lot anyway. One of her favorite pastimes is chasing rabbits when I go horse riding. Kizzie is great on photo shoots: she has a very calm temperament and is gentle with puppies, kittens, and babies! My little shadow.

Rachael Hale

Index

ISBN-13: 978-0-7407-7342-6
ISBN-10: 0-7407-7342-9
Library of Congress Control Number: 2007936192

This edition produced and originated by PQ Blackwell Limited,
116 Symonds Street, Auckland, New Zealand
www.pqblackwell.com

This edition published by Andrews McMeel Publishing, LLC,
4520 Main Street, Kansas City, Missouri 64111
www.andrewsmcmeel.com

Printed by Everbest Printing International Ltd, China.